Connect

Connecting with E.M. Forster
A Memoir

Tim Leggatt

For Penny,
Will, Eva & Jack
&
in memory of
Frank Kermode

Published by Hesperus Press Limited
28 Mortimer Street, London W1W 7RD
www.hesperuspress.com

Excerpts from E.M. Forster's *Locked Diary*, *Diary for 1958* and *Commonplace Book* are reproduced by kind permission of the Society of Authors as agent for the provost and the scholars of King's College, Cambridge.

Notes and introductory material from Philip Gardner's *Commonplace Book* (Scholar Press, 1988) and *The Journals and Diaries of E.M. Forster* (Pickering and Chatto, 2010) are reproduced by kind permission of the author.

First published by Hesperus Press Limited, 2012

Designed and typeset by Fraser Muggeridge studio
Printed in Jordan by Jordan National Press

ISBN: 978-1-84391-375-7

CONTENTS

PREFACE

This is a memoir of the last fifteen years of Forster's life, 1955–70, from the age of seventy-six to his death at the age of ninety-one, the years that I knew him. It is principally an account of my relationship with him during this period.

It is based on a number of sources: his more than a hundred letters to me; the fifteen letters from me to him that he chose to keep and quite possibly re-read; my journals of travelling with Forster, and on my own; and my memories.

I have also dipped into his *Commonplace Book*, published in 1985; his major diary, known as *The Locked Diary*, published in 2011; and, his *Journal* for 1958, published in the same year (both of these in the King's College archives). I have done this when he writes about my or Bob Buckingham's family or other significant people in his life; his health or his thoughts about dying; or his looking back over a past year.

In these years I was travelling a great deal and I also had several holidays with Forster. In the summer of 1956 I was on the island of Capri, and in the summer of 1957 in Nova Scotia, Canada. In 1958 we took a holiday in Italy, visiting Venice, Ravenna and Florence. Also in 1958 I went to India, where I lived in Calcutta (now Kolkata) and visited Bombay (now Mumbai), Bhubaneswar and Darjeeling. I returned to England in 1959. In 1960 I went to Ghana, and on leave from there in 1961 we took a holiday in August in Herefordshire. I left Ghana in 1962, and in the same year we took our second holiday in Italy: to Milan, Bergamo, Verona, Vicenza, Mantua and Padua. In 1964–6 I was in the United States, at the University of Chicago.

In this period Forster was much concerned about the world's growing population and the disappearance of the world in which he had been brought up, especially of the countryside.

I have digressed just once: to comment on the question as to why he wrote no more novels after *A Passage to India*, published in 1924.

I believe that I have given a fair and full account of Morgan Forster as I knew him. The greatest artistic celebration of King's College, Cambridge, where I met Morgan and still remember him, is Wordsworth's sonnet about King's Chapel.

Tax not the royal Saint with vain expense,
With ill-match'd aims the Architect who plann'd
(Albeit labouring for a scanty band
Of white-robed Scholars only) this immense

And glorious work of fine intelligence!
Give all thou canst; high Heaven rejects the lore
Of nicely-calculated less or more: –
So deemed the man who fashion'd for the sense

These lofty pillars, spread that branching roof
Self-poised, and scoop'd into ten thousand cells
Where light and shade repose, where music dwells

Lingering – and wandering on as loth to die;
Like thoughts whose very sweetness yieldeth proof
That they were born for immortality.

ACKNOWLEDGMENTS

I am grateful to Philip Gardner, editor of Forster's *Commonplace Book*, his *Locked Diary* and his *Journal* (1958), for his permission to quote from these publications and even their footnotes, which I have also supplemented from the internet.

I am grateful to Peter Jones, librarian of King's College, Cambridge, for permission to quote from the Forster archives, held by the college; and especially to Patricia McGuire, archivist at King's for her continuing help and encouragement.

My special thanks are due to Jonathan Miller and to my wife, Penny Smith, for their very constructive criticisms of my draft, which led to the memoir being both more focused and far better organised than it otherwise would have been. Responsibility for its final shape is of course entirely my own.

INTRODUCTION

When I went up to Cambridge in 1954, Morgan Forster was Britain's most distinguished writer. The only other great writers of the twentieth century were all dead: D.H. Lawrence had died in 1930, James Joyce and Virginia Woolf in 1941. Somerset Maugham, who lived until 1965, was a writer who had, and knew, his limits. Forster indeed had no rivals.

His output was admittedly unusual. He published five novels, of which his fifth and last, *A Passage to India*, appeared in 1924, when he was forty-five. He wrote his novel about homosexuals, *Maurice*, in 1913-4, but it was not published until after his death in 1971. Most of his short stories were published by 1928, although a further volume was published posthumously in 1972.

He wrote two biographies, of his friend and teacher Goldsworthy Lowes Dickinson in 1934, and of his aunt Marianne Thornton in 1956; and an Indian memoir, *The Hill of Devi*, in 1953. He shared with Eric Crozier the writing of the libretto for Benjamin Britten's *Billy Budd* in 1951.

He published a great many essays and reviews and made many broadcasts and speeches, often as a spokesman for the National Council of Civil Liberties and other liberal causes. He was president of the NCCL and also president of the Cambridge Humanists (from 1959 to 1970).

He was what he set out to be, a creative artist of great distinction.

However, he was not only an outstanding writer. He was also to those who took an interest in such things a significant homosexual. He had his first full relationship in Egypt in 1917 and there were many people in his circle and among his friends who were homosexuals: W.H. Auden, Benjamin Britten,

Constantine Cavafy, Christopher Isherwood, John Maynard Keynes, T.E. Lawrence, Siegfried Sassoon, and Lytton Strachey. So too were his closest friends: Joe Ackerley, Bob Buckingham, American actors Tom Coley and Bill Roerick, William Plomer, Jack Sprott; and, in the last decade of his life, Mattei Radev. When I arrived at King's, it was accepted throughout Cambridge that the college welcomed and contained many homosexuals, despite the fact that relations between consenting adults remained illegal until 1967.

And so it was that Morgan was not infrequently drawn to undergraduates through a homosexual interest, with the hope that a full relationship might develop. I was one of these, as were two other undergraduates mentioned in the following memoir, Brian Remnant and Lindsay Heather. Nothing came of these hopes. I was always firmly heterosexual and discussed such relationships more intimately with Morgan than with anyone else. My friend Jonathan Miller suggests that by virtue of me not being homosexual, Morgan was drawn to me more strongly than he would otherwise have been – because I was inaccessible. He continued to have sexual feelings to a great age. Jonathan also believes that, to Morgan, I was a Cyril Fielding (as in *A Passage to India)*, when I went to India, in a life that reminded him of Fielding's, and as a result was of special importance to him.

As he got older, he was much concerned with death, with how other people met theirs, and with how he would meet his. This too is evident in this memoir.

In my third year in King's, 1956–7, I had rooms next to Morgan's, where meetings of the Cambridge Apostles regularly took place, and I shared a bathroom with him. From that year my relationship with him was exceptionally close. It is something for which I will always be grateful.

I should note that I returned to King's as a fellow, 1973–82. I was senior tutor of the college, 1973–81.

Connecting with E.M. Forster
A Memoir

Morgan's mother died in March 1946, and he was asked to leave their house in West Hackhurst in Surrey. At this point he heard from John Sheppard,[1] the provost of King's, that he had been elected to an honorary fellowship, and, following swiftly upon this news, came an invitation to 'reside' in college. And so he did from the age of 67, for the remainder of his life.

I was the son of a naval officer with a fine war record, and his wife, the daughter of an admiral, and was thus as middle class as Morgan. I was educated at Eton, which I enjoyed rather more than Morgan enjoyed Tonbridge. I left in 1952, and for my two years of national service was commissioned in to the Rifle Brigade. I served in Germany in 1953-4. I arrived at King's, aged twenty, in 1954, and almost immediately joined the Ten Club, which met regularly to read plays. As I remember it, one was given a part to read at the start of each evening and then we read the play. There was, however, both before and after the reading, an opportunity to talk to and get to know those present.

It was over the course of several Ten Club meetings that I met and came to know Morgan, who, like myself, attended regularly. It seems likely that each year he wanted to meet the new undergraduates who had some interest in literature, and to see if any attracted him.

Locked Diary, 21 April
King's Chapel

Back little more than a week from Greece I went into the chapel[2] today while the light was fading and the organ playing Bach and felt I had stumbled back into a world which had taken the wrong turning after Christ, and had tried to explain human suffering by the <u>doctrine</u> of suffering, redemption, and atonement, and had identified heavenly happiness with rest. The Greeks did not solve our troubles as was sometimes dreamily hoped, their wars were horrible and endless, they were greedy and unkind. But they did not impose a false solution as Christianity has, and as Bach, burbling and buzzing through endless variations on a chorale, would confirm. The scene was magnificent – brownish light poured through the west window and converted the stone to sandstone, and picked over the niches and emphasised their different altitudes, and from the east a black tun-nel advanced and swallowed the fan vaulting. I was in the greatest building of the fifteenth century.

9 May
Various deaths

During the last six or five months, Johnny Simpson has died, Agnes has died, Ivor Ramsay threw himself from the top of the chapel on mother's birthday, Stephen Glanville (Provost here) died a fortnight back in a twinkling, Sydney Wilkinson has not recovered from her operation, Patrick (she told me yesterday) has injured his hip-socket and will be permanently lame, Kenneth Harrison's father is going dotty so that K (my best friend in King's) may have to leave Cambridge to look after him.[3]

None of the above people I dislike, most of them I love, and the cumulative reaction on me is not sadness, but indifference to the young. It has come on me suddenly and might have anyhow. I have lost the quick warmth that used to accompany their approach or the expression of their opinions. I do not find this in Bob,[4] whom I have mummified for my self preservation.

Commonplace Book, July
Himself and death

It is wrong to think one has to say something. It may be wrong to think one has something to say. An old author who is beginning his last book, as here I am, is depressed by the little effect his opinions have had – he might as well have never expressed them – and he is tempted to a last minute emphasis or to a filling up of gaps, which will make his purpose clearer. Vain effort – actually due to the shortness of time ahead of him, and to the sense of time wasted behind him. It is not to extend my influence that I am writing now, nor even to help. It is an attempt to be more honest with myself than I yet have, though such attempts usually defeat themselves through the self-consciousness they generate.

My life after death is unlikely to come in – though it might be if I was badly frightened. The belief that I may live after my breath ceases and my body begins to smell never occurs to me – either in the simple form cherished by my ancestors, or in the difficult modern ecclesiastical form, where the spiritual expert rebuffs the claimants to immortality, and convicts them of crudeness, and of unspirituality. I think of death as a permanent anaesthetic – to be reached amidst pain or fear if my luck is bad, and under perfect hospital conditions if the luck's good. In either case it finishes me off as a memoirist or an observer. My great extension is not through time to eternity, but through space to infinity: here: now: and one of my complaints against modern conditions is that they prevent one from seeing the stars.

By the end of my second year, in the summer of 1956, I already knew Morgan quite well.

Locked Diary, 4 August
Brian Remnant

Remnant[5] – will this funny name mean anything to me in two years time when I may next see him again, hardened and smartened by the RAF? I said a little when he went, very little, and that because I could not help it, too little for him to understand. His full-faced freshness, blue eyed, straight-staring courtesy: profile undistinguished. Myself – what a distinguished old man, and what I look like to him a glance at a looking glass must remind me. We were together from 4 to 6, and in incompatible ways happy.

Being a scholar, not a passing plough boy though he resembles one I may meet him again – coarsened, begirled, and lost, unless the feeling in me has struck a spark in him: unless his awe and excitement can be reborn as affection. If he was coming up in Oct. I should be in an odd state. He brought a cake from his mother to placate the oracle.

25 August
The Pleasures of Eroticism and Kenneth Harrison

For about a month – i.e. ever since I tried to conclude the

Unwritten Novel[6] – I have been controlled by erotic thoughts instead of controlling them, and I wish to record this unpleasant and disquieting experience, to the postponement of other work. I can not imagine a Catholic or other Religious reading this entry with trained sympathy or acquired contempt. For I do not <u>want</u> to be without the thoughts, however dirty they are, only to control them, and to stop them slipping into my mind in the form of half-sentences, hour after hour, until they tire it. The Christian way out of this is Confession, Absolution, Abnegation, and that it may work I do acknowledge. But it would leave me without any of the pleasures of eroticism, and I do not want to sacrifice them. I want to have them in their amusing and helpful warmth, but intermittently. How is this to be done? Neither solitude nor companionship is a cure. The proper preventive is work, and it is only since *Marianne Thornton*[7] has been finished, and the Unfinished Novel won't finish that the trouble's been a serious one.

This masturbational eroticism has had its conveniences. At all events I don't go hanging about urinals or showing my aged genitals to girls. It has also its inconveniences and I hope to minimise them. When I done [sic] my broadcasting script I will try to finish the adventure of Lionel and Cocoanut[8], and then I will go for a week to Holland.

I reopen book to enter events of day. Unimportant-seeming they may add up in the future. Most poignant is the return of Kenneth from York, ill-tempered and overtired. He has been preparing to move his dotty dad. K. my best friend in King's. Does he know this? I do not remember anything that has been said – except Kenneth's petulance against literary people, and the bitterness against the marriages which have robbed him of his friends. 50/50. It has rained on and off, cold between times.

Since Morgan knew me quite well, and since Kenneth Harrison, who had the rooms next door to his, was taking a sabbatical year in 1956–7, Morgan was invited to choose an undergraduate to be his neighbour for that year. He chose me. This came of course as a great surprise, but it was one which delighted me. I was fond of Morgan, and it was a rare privilege to be given rooms that were normally reserved for a fellow, next to his.

The rooms were immense by undergraduate standards. I had my own bedroom with an iron bedstead, which I had to climb up into. I shared a bathroom with Morgan, and I had a palatial living room-cum-study, looking across the front court to the chapel, so that I could hear the organ scholar practising in the evenings, as the sound of the organ was wafted across the court. This room was next to Morgan's room, in which the Apostles[9] met.

Forster in his rooms in King's, mid-1950s.

However, before moving into Kenneth's rooms, I had my second long vacation to take and this was when my exchange of letters with Morgan began. Whenever I was abroad, our letters to each other were quite lengthy, while those written in England were almost always very short, simply about arrangements to meet in London or Cambridge. I kept every one of Morgan's, more than a hundred letters, and he kept fifteen of mine.

Why did he keep these particular letters? I believe it was because they either concerned my intimate relationships – invariably with girls – and told him something about me, or because I expressed great affection for him. I assume that he may have read some of these again.

In the summer of 1956 I took a job on the island of Capri as tutor to two Italian boys, to teach them English – one of them having an exam to take in September. The family was rich and aristocratic, a prince and princess, and my stay had its interest and gave me many tales to tell. I met through them a great range of people, from Renato Rascel, author of the pop song *Arrivederci Roma*, to the film star, Nadia Gray; and through a peeress from the north of England, who was holidaying on Capri, the novelists Curzio Malaparte and Alberto Moravia.[10]

I have of course wondered if Morgan saw this trip as the equivalent of his visit to the Countess Elizabeth von Arnim in 1905.[11]

I seem not to have written to Morgan until the end of my two months' stay.

TWL to EMF, 31 August
I thought that I would not write to you until I had some clearly-formed impressions and opinions about this place, until I had got beneath the touristy skin to the bones below. But things haven't turned out so simply as that; perhaps

they never do. I had hoped that, despite my apprehensions – shared with you – about the restrictions of life here, about living in an unknown rich aristocratic family, about staying two and a half months, despite all this, yet I would be rewarded by a fascinating study of an unknown way of life and strange people provided only I kept my eyes and sensibilities open. Well, either I'm not observant enough or else – my ideas about southern strangeness and 'unknown life', etc. were rather over-romantic and wide of the mark. At any rate Capri has palled, and some days ago I gave notice to the princess, cutting fourteen days off my stay here.

My main trouble has been the horror of the children with whom I'm obliged to live a twelve-hour day: or rather the younger of the two. They're both spoilt to a degree that I had never imagined before. They have never heard the word 'no', they have never been reprimanded let alone punished for anything. The younger, aged eleven, is the most selfish, rude, petulant, foul-mouthed[12] (this is horrifying) and elaborately dishonest boy I've ever met. He begs money from all the guests in the house, and steals it from his parents. He takes his father's cigarettes. He never tells the truth. I don't myself think that there's any way of improving him, let alone curing. And this is why. His father is the same and intends willy-nilly to bring the boy up in this way. He gives him everything, tells everyone how wonderful and clever and talented he is, tells the boy so. The mother is horrified, and fears that the elder boy will eventually hate his father for this favouritism. The elder is lazy and irritable but he believes the best of people, makes excuses for his brother and is very sensitive. All too much so. He'll, I'm afraid, be a most unhappy person.

As to the parents, the mother is Roman, deeply religious, strictly brought up, incredibly neurotic, weak (in character) and invariably worn out. (I've still said nothing directly to her about leaving. Everything has to be done through a third party, she's too nervous to talk to me.) The marriage has collapsed – the rift now widens continually over the problem child – and must have been fated from the start: indeed so it was, for the princess's family cut her off when she first married. The husband is a conceited Neapolitan nobleman going to fat and to seed. Always a good-for-nothing he has the money to keep himself so. He's bad-tempered, cruel, dishonest and fatuously concerned about always being in the limelight.

It is a difficult family to live with, but it has been an experience to be a servant and observe life from this angle.

My second trouble has been having no second life to offset the strain of the first. During my working day I never meet anyone under forty – another thing which is hardly good for the boys – and I'm not free till 10 p.m. And then, tired and irritable, I just meander alone. Of course, I've read, and written letters and a diary, and met the odd person, but still no one of my age and after seven weeks it became an additional strain.

It's possible I'll visit Cambridge just for one day in September, when I shall certainly come to see you. Either then, or later, I'll have much to talk about. Having got so far, I suddenly cannot launch into my feelings about Capri itself.

I hope you've survived this horrible summer in England. For me it's hard even to imagine.

I need not have worried about the older boy's English exam. He took it near Naples and the Prince paid the examiner so much before the exam and so much when the boy's pass was announced. I was told that the princess was quite ignorant of this arrangement.

And so I left Capri and had a delightful time in Rome, staying with one of the Princess's friends whom I had met on Capri. I explored Rome and its outskirts on a motor scooter, undoubtedly the best way to do it.

In July, Egypt, under President Nasser, nationalised the Suez Canal, and thus started what became known as the Suez Crisis.

Morgan wrote to me on 14 September from Leiden,[13] where he was staying with Dutch friends.

I am abroad myself, though scarcely in your surroundings, and I must send you a line to thank you for your most interesting letter.

Your experience is what's called 'most valuable', but it could have been just as valuable if it had lasted two and a half weeks instead of months, and I don't doubt that you are regretting the losses in temper and time. I hope you kept some sort of diary, for what you got across to me is quite out of the way. I was a servant myself for three months when I was your age, but under more normal circumstances, and I got on with the other servants.

I've hauled myself out here for a week's change. It is a pleasant place but as it is a university town on which rain falls constantly, the change is not a marked one. I stay near Dutch friends who kindly drive me about. The absence of sun certainly has been appalling and has got everyone down, and I think may have had political consequences: people who would otherwise have done some thinking about Suez and Cyprus have become too sogged to operate.

Tomorrow we see the Rembrandt exhibition at Rotterdam, Sunday we lunch at the Roman Catholic University of Nijmegen, Monday at this university (Protestant). The outgoing rector inducts the ingoing with a forty-five minute speech in Dutch, ending however with the words 'Salve, Rector Magnifice, dunque Salve'. It is for the sake of these words and of the sherry that succeeds them that I am attending.

I returned to Cambridge, to the rooms next to Morgan, to the start of my third year, which was overshadowed by the Hungarian Revolution, which broke out on 23 October, and by the ongoing Suez crisis – Britain, France and Israel invaded Egypt in the last days of October.

At the Founder's Feast[14] in December 1956, I sat next to Morgan, when Noel Annan,[15] the provost, made a speech in which he looked back over the recent history of the college. At one point, he said how delighted the college had been to welcome 'Britain's greatest living novelist' to live within it. Some minutes later, I asked Morgan if he hadn't been embarrassed by these words, 'Oh no,' he said, 'not at all!' He may usually have appeared very diffident, but he always reverted to a good opinion of his worth as a great novelist and a great artist.

Commonplace Book, 1957
The Paris Review

'As for living novelists I suppose E.M. Forster is the best, not knowing what there is, but at least he's a semi-finalist, wouldn't you think? Somerset Maugham once said to me, "We have a novelist here, E.M. Forster, though I don't expect he's familiar to you." Well I could have kicked him. Did he think I carried a papoose on my back? Why I'd go on my hands and knees to get to Forster. He wrote once something I've always remembered: "It has never happened to me that I've had to choose between betraying a friend and betraying my country, but if it ever does so happen I hope I have the guts to betray my country." Now doesn't that make the Fifth Amendment look like a bum.'

Dorothy Parker,[16] interviewed in the *Paris Review*[17] gave the above agreeable surprise. Has she not dusted over and failed? I have not read her lately and she sounds out at elbows.

In 1956–7 I was working towards my Finals, working quite hard, though very much distracted by my relationship with a very intelligent Hungarian refugee, who subsequently obtained a Cambridge doctorate. I had a very close relationship with her, and then lost touch in the autumn of 1957. She came into my life again many years later.

I took my final exams in the summer of 1957 and immediately left for Canada – even before graduation – to work for a paper company based in Liverpool, Nova Scotia. I feel sure that I wrote to Morgan while my friend Garry and I,[18] whose father had arranged the job, spent eleven weeks working in the Nova Scotian woods on a survey of the trees from which newspaper is made.

Morgan wrote me a delightful letter on 3 August:

If we don't take care we shall never write to each other, which would be a pity, so here is a line though I don't know your address and have not indeed much to say. The visit to Austria with the Buckinghams is my show-bit of news I suppose; a crowded and rewarding fortnight during which I sometimes felt hot and tired. Climax in Vienna (to which we went in a boat down the Danube) – where my one Austrian friend has been so good as to become head of all the antiquities and monuments in his country. This meant having a super-guide to the museums, churches, castles, sceneries, and the only difficulty is now, when we are trying to sort them out, and keep ten baroque abbeys and twelve Breughels apart.

Here at Cambridge the chief piece of news is a mouse, which I saw dancing in our bathroom fender, and the very same morning Mr Schofield[19] saw a second mouse upstairs. This was a graver matter. It resulted in the arrival of a rodent-exterminator, a trim grey-haired military-looking man whom the bed-makers found irresistible. I detested him. He ascribed the invasion to the Hungarian underneath, who occupies one of Pigou's[20] rooms. 'Dirt, sir – Central Europe and similarly the Middle East, and they don't like it when you tell them of it.' Then he put down some crystals, and the smell of rodents who have been exterminated in the wainscot is gradually gathering strength. Two have been found entangled in Mrs Blackwell's lavatory brush.

You see the dimensions of my news: mice. There are probably actually rats in Canada and rat-catchers who catch them, and I look forward to a reply on the grand scale. I haven't much gossip of the human sort, and am indeed not good at accumulating it. (You are usually reported as knowing a good deal and not passing it on.) Norman[21] – to go to the other extreme – exults in his hush-hush work at the observatory and is now off for six weeks to the States. Ian Stephens[22] shakes off our dust permanently in order to reside at Rawalpindi and write the official history of the Pakistani Army. He will enjoy this and be among people whom he likes, but a less rewarding and I must add a more foolish job I find it hard to imagine. He won't even be able to tell the truth.

I am so glad that your own work seems opening in such an interesting and promising way, and wish you good fortune in it. The snag should be the difference between your political attitude and that of your colleagues and superiors – the more different since the politics are likely to be foreign politics. I haven't myself any great quarrel with the Conservatives over home affairs. Sometimes they seem to me right. It's when they look abroad that they go wrong and are bound to do so – especially when they look at non-white people.

I have just written a small article on old age which is rather funny, unlike most essays on that solemn subject and will someday appear in the *London Magazine*. I am now reviewing a *Life of Harriet Martineau*, and you may imagine me falling asleep over it in the Fellows' Garden.

No one is in your room for the moment. Kenneth should return to it in the next month. A pity you are not both there. You have between you made my life here very pleasant, and I am grateful indeed.

When I left the work in the paper company, I had saved sufficient money to enable me to visit family in Ottawa and friends – two Old Kingsmen – in Washington and New York. I then returned to Canada, to Dalhousie in New Brunswick, for the return voyage. On 11 October – I think the day before leaving – I wrote Morgan a letter summing up my time in Canada and the States.

I finally worked for eleven weeks in Liverpool, Nova Scotia, longer than I had originally intended. My work was in the woods but it was not cutting trees; nor did I live in bunk-houses with heavy-forearmed giants. Together with Garry, I worked with two Canadian graduates, at survey work. This meant plunging through the woods in straight lines recording the growth of the trees. Though sometimes it was quite hard work, in the main it was rather monotonous like all other totally unskilled jobs. I don't believe it mattered greatly not being in the bunk-houses because even there life isn't as rugged as one's fevered English imagination leads one to believe. I realise now that I had put lumber-camps second only to the Foreign Legion for toughness. What folly! If each man has a house, a car, a T.V. set, a washing-machine, etc., why on earth should anyone need to gamble, drink, brawl and what-have-you? The pioneer spirit likewise is totally out of place in the midst of prosperity and security, where no one ever walks unless his car breaks down. What a change it was, therefore, to live in a country where there are no classes and no grave social and economic problems: I am meaning here from the individual's point of view, not Mr Diefenbaker's.

All this accounts quite largely for what impressed me most in Canada – the quite exceptional friendliness of absolutely everyone. No kindness put them out, and I blush to think that they regard as normal what to us is extreme friendliness. On the one hand there is the contrast with Britain, and on the other with the States. There I found that people in restaurants and shops were gruff, and so steely-eyed and intimidating that I kept finding myself cowed into buying some unwanted trifle just so as to make my escape. Also of course there is the characteristic American bonhomie which jars on the Englishman because seeming to him over-exuberant and skin-deep. Quite rightly so in my opinion, but not because of insincerity. It seems to me that the American assumes this manner of his not for the benefit of foreigners, but in a desperate attempt to cope with his own countrymen, who are – as I'm sure you know, but I didn't – more various and more strange to each other than one can possibly imagine without experience of them.

I am glad that I worked so long in the one place. It was only, I would say, in my eighth week that I really began to get assimilated to the community. I ended up having made a number of genuine friends and with quite a fair idea of how people live and what they think in one part of Canada. It is irrelevant that Nova Scotia is regarded as a backwater. It is still Canada. And beyond this I had three weeks experience of living in a small town, in Liverpool itself. Everybody there worked in the paper mill, so they lived and worked together. Rather grisly because so very gossipy: at the same time stable because self-contained.

After all this, I had three and a half weeks' holiday. With so little time I could not explore, but visited only places where I had friends. First Ottawa, pleasant but dull. Then Toronto, but only for two days. Next Washington, where I stayed with an Old Kingsman. This I greatly enjoyed. There are some delightful houses, a National Gallery full of European masterpieces, and a sense of history in the atmosphere. I was driven out into the Virginian countryside, very lovely, and saw some old houses and civil war battlefields.

My final visit was to New York, which I found stimulating and exhausting. What a varied, many-sided place! I sightsaw furiously, up skyscrapers, round museums, in and about odd places. What colour there is over there – in the houses and cars and everywhere. And what a splurging, an exhibition of energy which we in Europe hoard, treasure and channel so carefully. Perhaps this goes hand in hand with money consciousness which obtrudes everywhere. Where else does one man give away $8,000,000, as Rockefeller did to the U.N.? It has been most exciting and refreshing. I have never been so carefree: for my work prevented money troubles. Still, I shall not be sorry to be back – with the old values and the comparative calm.

On my return to England, I started work with the P&O Shipping Company. I was to spend a year in London before going out to work for seven years in shipping agencies in Calcutta and further east: but, at the end of the period, I wasn't guaranteed a job with the company, although I was told that I would 'be able to get a job anywhere in British shipping'.

During the year I saw a great deal of Morgan in London or Cambridge. In London, I frequently met him at the Reform Club, for lunch or dinner, and stayed in his flat in Chiswick. He wrote on 22 November, of one such meeting:

We did have a good conversation that evening. It is curious how talk suddenly becomes interesting, and the possibility that it may become so is one of the reasons for talking.

EMF to TWL, 9 January

New Year's Day I spent at Quarter Sessions, sitting in the gallery with the mates and mums of the gangsters who were being tried. We were all very polite. Every gangster had a mum who extricated herself from our tangle and went into the witness box to testify to her son's character. She never did any good. Nor could I feel the judge's harshness un-justified – though I wondered, if he came to be tried, what would be said of him.

Morgan was very philosophical about my going to India. Indeed I think that he enjoyed the thought of me going to a country that he so much loved. On 6 May he wrote:

I am sure one ought to get away from home at your age, no matter to what. I did not do so, and it was a mistake. But it was specially difficult, for my mother would have been left alone. I had no second parent nor any married brother in the offing.

We'll talk when we meet. It was a most pleasant cruise. It lacked the glamour of its predecessor, but I have brought back plenty of good health from it and memories of scenery and objects, varying in size from Mount Athos to a gold mask.

He refers of course to his very long mutual dependence with his mother, of the great length of time that he lived with her.

Thoughts on his novels

Howards End: my best novel and approaching a good novel. Very elaborate and all-pervading plot that is seldom tiresome or forced, Range of characters, social sense, wit, wisdom, colour. Have only just discovered why I don't care for it: not a single character in it for whom I care. In *Where Angels*, Gino; in *L.J.*, Stephen; in *R. with V.*, Lucy; in *P. To I.*, Aziz ... and Maurice, and Alec ... and Lionel and Cocoa ... perhaps the house in *H.E.,* for which I once did care, took the place of people and now that I no longer care for it their barrenness has become evident. I feel pride in the achievement, but cannot love it, and occasionally the swish of the skirts and the non-sexual embraces irritate.

Perhaps too I am more hedonistic than I was, and resent not being caused pleasure personally.

Journal, 10 May
Eightieth Birthday, deafness

Two surprises: (i) The Council, via Noel, offer me a great eightieth birthday luncheon on 9 Jan., 1959. I think I shall accept it rather than the two smaller alternatives. (ii) I have gone deaf in the right ear. I always knew that old age troubles would come unexpectedly, but am no less surprised. It may be wax but I do not think so. I noticed it, without doing so, about a week ago. It was proved in my sitting room a couple of hours ago, when, if I closed my left ear, I couldn't hear the clock tick.

Before I left Cambridge, Morgan and I planned to take a proper holiday together – in Italy. His letter of 13 June, after the King's May Ball, noted:

The Ball was a great success for all including me, who slept peacefully through the jazz band in the Reading Room. The girls' dresses looked lovely through the misty darkness, wish I could have looked at them more closely, but had to slink about pretending to be a detective.

On 8 July he was thinking about me going to India:

I liked two of the bits of your news – namely that you have talked with someone sympathetic in the higher ranks of the P&O command, and that you are going to Bombay instead of Calcutta. The Bengalis are very good for one but no comfort, also Elephanta[23] is one of the very great things in India and the world, greater even than its reputation. Atmosphere and entourage come in, both are unstable and perhaps I was lucky, for on my last visit – the one that counts in my memory – I was almost alone with the heavens also quiet and the gash in the hill side, through which the images are visible, fringed with creepers.

In fact, I did go to Calcutta and, alas, I never went to Elephanta.

Journal, 14 July
Mohammed
Strongest re-experience for a long time. Took out Mohammed's letters from the File of the Dead with the intention of destroying them unread, glanced, and was overwhelmed.[24] What a fine boy, what charm, seriousness and faithfulness.

EMF to Benjamin Britten, 27 August

[T]his trend of our days, which are so depressing – not because one will die or even because one's friends will, but because the human race seems advancing to disaster via vulgarity. It is very difficult to see anything great in the general movement of the last ten years. Science might be wonderful, but it is applied so contemptibly that one is disgusted or bored: the mucky doings on the bed of the sea, the attempt to land on the moon in the hope of finding something there which might hurt another human being on the earth drive one back to the act of creation as the only possible escape. Unfortunately one doesn't create by being driven, but I do hope you will evolve something that will help you and others to see what we are moving into.

I hope… I may not be caught in a moment of terror and fear to deny my unbelief and to become additional propaganda for the believists.

At the end of August we took our long awaited holiday in Italy, flying to Milan, and visiting Venice, Ravenna and Florence. In Venice we found a modest *pensione* as a base from which to see some of the outstanding buildings and paintings. It was a friendly place, and I remember talking, in my best Italian, to a man wearing a shirt that I liked, to ask him where he bought it.

We had, as our guide, *Baedeker's Northern Italy* (1913), but it was in fact Morgan's memory of places that he had especially enjoyed that determined where we went. Nevertheless, we still enjoyed the Baedeker with passages such as this quotation from Ruskin on the Church of San Marco:

The effects of St Mark's depend not only upon the most delicate sculpture in every part, but, as we have just stated, eminently on its colour also, and that the most subtle, variable, inexpressible colour in the world, the colour of glass, of transparent alabaster, of polished marble, and lustrous gold.

TWL, Venice Journal
I cannot now make this into a day by day journal. It is already the third day's end. When I can, I shall try to shape the tumble of emotions that I have been and am feeling. I am so utterly confused. I started out in a dejected and lost spirit, and I had not in any way begun to think about my holiday. So all my impressions surge upon me before I can understand or control them, least of all order them.

I hadn't realised that Morgan would walk so slowly [he was 79] and that we should have to take taxis with merciless extravagance to avoid having to walk.

I was evidently at times a discontented and grumbling tourist:

I so despise myself for going about gawking at buildings which don't move me. With paintings it is somehow different, because they are visions of life or observations upon it. But a long procession of churches is physically debilitating. Of course some architecture has an immediate and moving impact. It is looking in a corner of an apse or in the third chapel off to the right for a gloomy painting by some little known Paduan artist that bores me stiff and sets my guts knotting themselves in resentment.

And I seriously missed the company of women.

This evening in the Piazzetta & Piazza di San Marco I could have cried aloud. It was such an extreme sentimental atmosphere, such a perfect place for gaiety and love. I felt insupportably alone. I seem to feel this far too often. I'm becoming maudlin. But Venice is so lovely and strange. And even the slap of the water against the riva outside is warm and friendly as well as so firm and inevitable.

Outside the church of San Marco, with its four bronze horses pillaged from Byzantium, the Palazzo Ducale and the Accademia, we particularly enjoyed the magnificent Carpaccios in the Scuola San Giorgio degli Schiavoni and, myself, the Tintorettos in the Scuola Grande di San Rocco. We also saw the great statue of Bartolemeo Colleoni by Andrea del Verrochio, of which Ruskin wrote, 'I do not believe there is a more glorious work of sculpture existing in the world than the equestrian statue of Bartolemeo Colleoni' (Baedeker). In the same square were the Dominican church of Santi Giovanni e Paolo, Venice's most famous church after San Marco, crowded with works of art; and the barrel-roofed 'marble church' of Santa Maria dei Miracoli.

At the Accademia we met Rose Macaulay,[25] sublimely dignified, and the rather fussy Stephen Spender.[26] One of the highest points of our visit was going to the Teatro La Fenice, an absolutely exquisite theatre. We heard Stravinsky himself conducting the music of *The Rite of Spring*.

We rounded off our trip to Venice with a boat tour to Murano – with its glass, Burano – with its Venetian lace, and Torcello (grotesquely hurried), with its wonderful twelfth-century Byzantine mosaics.

TWL, Venice Journal
I am to a small extent discomforted by the thought that Morgan's affection for me has its roots in homosexuality –

however natural that may be. Possibly this brings about the tepidity of his philosophy, but that is being harsh. It is gentleness not tepidity. Strange somehow that he thinks marriage the most important thing in a man's life, or rather having children – which isn't so strange.

There are one or two glimpses of my own that I shall remember. On arrival at the station at Venice a great brown group of heavy monks – all wearing white topees. In the tiny square behind our Venetian *pensione* an assault of fluffy whirring pigeons.

Next we moved to Ravenna, where we particularly enjoyed the fifth-century mosaics in the Battistero degli Ortodossi and the Mausoleum of Galla Placidia, as well as the church of San Vitale.

TWL, Venice Journal
The Ravenna mosaics were knock-out. In the past mosaics have just been wide-eyed figures staring from glossy pages in expensive book-shops. Suddenly, a new world of beauty opened. The figures lived, sparkled, gloriously coloured, moving, with an endless complexity of appearance.

The journey from Ravenna to Florence via Faenza was very lovely. The country, intensely cultivated where possible, beginning as tiny knobs of foothills, merging into sharply cut incisive peaks and dells, becoming slowly more mountain-ous, furry with green trees. Small country scenes were visible, including, yes, the yeoman taking his horses to drink from the low dried river.

The great bus that rushed me to Siena gave lovely views of gentle sloping hills, intensely cultivated.

I went to Siena by myself as Morgan was saving himself for Florence. In Siena I had a happy meeting with close friends who were on their honeymoon, and visited the Duomo and the Palazzo Pubblico. It was not until years later that I saw the Palio.

In Florence there was so much to see – the Galleria degli Uffizi, the Palazzo Pitti and the Palazzo del Bargello, for a start. In the Bargello we loved Donatello's *David* and I very much took to Michelangelo's *Brutus.* He somehow captured the image of a thoughtful man who has worried over what to do (about Caesar) and has finally made up his mind, though with some misgiving and a heavy heart. Marvellous.

We also saw the Battistero di Duomo, the Medici Chapel and the Accademia di Bell'Arte. We were overwhelmed by gorgeous paintings of the very greatest artists. And on our return through Milan, we naturally took in the art gallery at the Palazzo di Brera.

TWL, Venice Journal
This is an oddly assorted glimpse into that packed fortnight, in which so much happened – at least in my mind. Morgan is surely the most complete and consistent person I know: the continuity of his life is staggering. I fell utterly in love with Italy – its country and culture, elegance and cleanliness, warmth and sparkle and language. It was a lovely holiday.

Afterwards, Morgan wrote, on 20 September:

That was a marvellous fortnight. I have come back feeling so well, thanks to your kindness and all the trouble you took. I loved your company, as you know, and I also had emotions which the Medusa of the Seguso[27] might well have denounced. Maybe you knew about that too. I mention it now because I wish you to know. There was no advantage in mentioning it earlier.

The taxi you got went as swiftly as the wind and much more intelligently. We were in good time for the train. When tipping the driver I congratulated him on the course he had taken, and he replied, 'I appreciate that remark very much indeed sir.' Quite like a bit of Italy. Not so my meal on the train, a filthy plateful of fried stuff which really made me heave. Not so my arrival in Cambridge where no one would carry my case. At last a very cross deaf man was induced to shout into the night: 'Mite, 'ere's a bloke wants a taxi' and the mite emerged.

College dead quiet, but illuminated for the Old Boys' Dinner. Half looked like a tomb, and Kenneth says felt like one, for Provost Sheppard and Sir Nevile Bland[28] both spoke at inordinate length and boringly. My rooms were all nice and comfortable, I slept well under three blankets instead of half a sheet, and today have had a fire.

I have started the wine and like it very much, but it fizzes slightly and may not be long for this world. I think I may as well eat the panforte too.

I replied, also in September:

It was a magnificent holiday for me too. Without you, not only would the means have been lacking – for which I have throughout been very grateful, but which I felt it would have been ill-judged to keep alluding to – but so too would the will to go: and on top of that the pleasure. I hope you were able to feel this.

I appreciate what you say about your feelings, which, yes, I had sensed. It seems you didn't find me difficult to live with. I feel it's an undertaking for anyone, because, as you saw, I do have terrible moods and when I'm in them I kill my companions' spirits and enthusiasms quicker than anyone. I thought you handled me with incomparable skill.

My wine too was fizzy, perhaps because of the journey. The figs were a huge success, only one was too soggy to be eaten. The panforte I thought rather dull and tough.

The trains are filthy and City lunches repulsive and most of the English sour. The odd exception is a delight. Then I suddenly think 'these wretched, grey-faced dank people really can't help it since they live in a wretched, grey, dank climate'. Still they do let it get them down.

Journal, 29 September

Rained all day, dark, warmish. Very content with my own company and pleasantly slack. Had fried plaice, cold mutton, green salad & potato salad in my room for dinner, also grapes and *panforte* and swigged away at a good grocer's wine, slightly fizzy, which Tim got at Milan. Have not yet posted my letter to him.

I wonder what the past fortnight will look like in a year's time. Shall I have forgotten the sunlight, the one sheet only at night, the delicious coffee, bread, confiture, veal, wine, and T's unusual torso as he sprawled half-stripped close to me doing 'our accounts'? All these items will shift their relationships and so get changed. It is odd that I don't mind him going to India for three years, never to be seen again by me, or if seen greatly changed. The curtain has fallen on a play of predestined length. As long as I live though I shall never forget it as a play – ending with that view from the plane of all Switzerland. I beautifully placed in a seat he thought was bad, beyond him an Italian from Udine, aged sixteen, who was going to Canada and had never eaten a sandwich before.

I haven't made an entry like this for a long time. I don't think I've got it in me to make many entries. Will swig a little more and retire. I cannot see it will do any harm to post the letter. During the fortnight it could have been dangerous.

EMF to TWL, 3 October
Your moods didn't worry me, Tim. They seemed more like moodlets to me, no doubt because of my age. Or (to put it more accurately, also more civilly) they never – however deep they may have gone – made me feel that I was responsible for them.

What I ought to apologise for is fidgeting. But I do assure you I was far worse fifty years ago.

Just off to London, second visit to the Byzantium Exhibition. I saw Rose Macaulay at the first one, and she expressed the wish that she had been permitted to see more of us in Venice.

EMF to TWL, 8 October
About a London meeting
We may have no other opportunity before your departure to talk in peace. There's the state of the world or parts of it, there's *Dr Zhivago* or parts of that and if we think it worth while there are the incredible letters S.S.[29] has written to me about Venice.

Journal, 25 October
On a memorial to Francis Bennett

Ignoble memorial service in Caius for our beloved.[30] Joe and Nick[31] came up for it. We wish we hadn't. A reach-me-down, taken off the peg for dead don after don. No attempt to please Francis in it, not even music he might have liked, and all the 'immortal-life' rubbish which the church is said else where to be scrapping. The utmost he thought is that something exciting <u>might</u> be waiting for us. I have never felt more hopeless and depressed in the presence of death. Never another memorial service – I now prefer funerals. I have so wanted to be comforted – unusual. I nearly cried.

Journal, 27 October
On deafness

I take up my pen to record my <u>deafness</u> while it is still fresh. In a short time I shall be used to it and have nothing to say. In company I have to repeat to everyone, right as well as left, 'I can't hear.'

But that is a trifle. The tragedy is the deformation of music. My lovely gramophone – just bought and intended to outlast my old age is almost incomprehensible. It was perfect two days ago. And if I strike a chord on the piano it is completely wrong yet I can't think how it is wrong. I have little hope of regaining my connection with music.

Tim asks me to see him off Thursday.

Have just been to tea with George Trevy,[32] deaf too, also blind and three years my senior. But he cheers me because he does <u>not</u> expect or even wish to see his much-liked wife after his death, and because he thinks we have come through the fifty worst years of history not too badly.

Must sleep. And no Francis to tell it to. He – and tho far after him – Johnny Simpson – are irreparable.

It is the day that I realise I can't hear music, because of increased distortion through deafness, so I have not been happy. I am determined not to be got down.

I am very glad I went to St Pancras yesterday. It was a good farewell, not that that is saying a lot. After leaving you I went down to dear little Sylvia Buckingham and her pleasing baby, and we all three lunched.

The news awaiting me at Cambridge was sad though – Rose Macaulay has suddenly died. I am so glad we had that glimpse of her outside the Accademia, so affectionate and happy, and I had another and similar glimpse at the Byzantine Exhibition. Of all the writers who are at all well known she must be by far the most beloved.

Our Stephen's latest has been to draft a long cable to the Union of Soviet Writers about their expulsion of Pasternak, and to ask for my support. Which I gladly gave, though I didn't care for the wording: too diffuse and hovering between patronage and coaxing – the sort of wording the Soviets must be accustomed to receive from the west. However by the time it reached them P must have refused the prize, and made them all feel very silly without any efforts on our part. I think better and better of him, don't you.

My London doctor's daughter has just taken a photograph of me, chattering the while modishly. I will see what I look like – I want you of course rather to look like what you looked like in Italy, but we shall remember our fortnight there without difficulty even if the photographs fail.

I left for India in November, to work in a shipping agency. I took a P&O ship to Bombay (now Mumbai) and then a train to Calcutta – in a first class carriage, of course – the only way for white people to travel.

TWL, Indian Journal
The view was always interesting, because so utterly new even if unvaried. The plains of India. Not desert, but sparsely cultivated rough land with the occasional people dotted around. Mud-hut villages, ragged and naked people wandering vaguely, with cattle, at the well, playing, just isolated, on their hunkers. Rather aimlessly scraping a bare subsistence from the ground. Just existing.

Then the Bengal countryside replaced the plains. Much greener, with trees thicker, rice fields, more people about. And suddenly Calcutta.

I found a strange life there. I had a job that I found boring, since it didn't require either brain power or human sympathy, and so had no rewards that I could detect. And socially it was much like *Jewel in the Crown* or even *A Passage to India.* The smartest club, the Tollygunge, was for whites only – and this was in 1958, when India's independence had come about in 1947. So too was the Calcutta Swimming Club, to which white but not black Americans were admitted. Whites and Indians did not readily mix socially, excepting only Indians who had risen in British commercial firms.

It is worth noting that although Morgan was criticised for describing the India of before the First World War in *A Passage to India* written in 1924, his India was still recognisable in 1958.

Thanks for your first impressions of Calcutta and I do hope your Indian contacts will persist and develop. I have just been to Ashok Desai; who had a remarkable young Indian from Trinity, plus his vina upon which he played, I should think at professional level.[33] Both hands were utterly deformed, claws of a tortured bird, and the contrast between them and the sounds they produced and his general graciousness made me feel that India and her products are still something quite out of the way.

The earlier part of the day was also out of the way, but not so pleasantly. I was televised. Five men were in my room for two and a half hours, taking shots which will be over in two and a half minutes. I came in. I sat. I wrote. I looked up to indicate inspiration. I took a book out of a book case. I read. When I left them they started televising the fire and throwing brightness into it from the flood lights they had affixed to long poles. I asked why this had to be. 'Oh you looked at the fire, we wanted to give the impression of it looking back'. They had great abilities. Tomorrow I say a few words about my work, the world, the dear old Coll, etc., and they will be pasted on to my face or my book case or the fire down in the studio, and will be administered to viewers on 4 January.

An appalling plaque of Stephen Glanville has appeared in the 'Cloisters'; bright gold, not like him, furnished with raised spectacles into which string or daisies could be threaded, and perched – crowning horror – on the top of a five polished slope of black stone, Tutankhemen style.

Everyone is furious and has signed a round robin to Noel, who, believe it or not, has bowed before the blast, and the bust will go back to its maker, and the stone slab, presumably, into the foundations of Churchill College.

I am looking forward to my birthday celebrations or some of them, but am unfortunately going deaf. You would not have noticed it on St Pancras. I'm all right with one person, but I've been to specialists and tried a hearing aid. I have given them up, because the thing that really annoyed me – the distortion of music – has certainly improved, probably through some psychological adjustment on my part, and I can enjoy my gramophone again, and don't mind saying 'What?' a bit.

It has been miserable about Rose (Macaulay), she was one of the very best. You will be pleased, Tim, that I had a further meeting with her at the Byzantine Exhibition, a very enjoyable one. Her death has set Stephen Spender off again and he has been wailing to Joe Ackerley that I never answered his letter and have not forgiven him. So now I have written and told him not to worry, which seems to work all right, but I wish I understood what forgiveness is. I don't seem capable of it. I can easily forget, or realise I was in the wrong or partly in it, but forgiveness seems to me something absolute, something godlike, or at least angelic, which I can't find inside me.

Forster, May Buckingham and Joe Ackerley, Shepherd's Bush, early 1950s.

TWL to EMF, 19 December

This is supposed to be a Christmas letter bringing my best Christmas wishes, but if, as I suspect, it comes too late, it can still inaugurate the epoch-making eightieth birthday year.

Thank you for your long letter. I enjoyed your description of the T.V. photographing; I'm sorry I shan't see it. Yes, I liked Lasham Gliding Centre's letter. It was gallant of them to take your word that the untraceable Mr Leggatt had paid.

I read, partly with amusement and partly with sympathy, that S.S. is still making overtures to you. It seems so remarkably petty to want your forgiveness in writing. He sounds so concerned that the right people should think just the right things about him.

You'll be amused to hear that I have a commission to write book reviews for a Calcutta newspaper called *The Hindustan Standard*. It plays second fiddle to *The Statesman* but I think it's more enterprising, even though the standard of journalism is desperately low. Well, isn't it good? I've written one review so far, of Brendan Behan's *Borstal Boy*, a roisterous vernacular account of his prison experiences (banned in Ireland as obscene – on account of the language). It was well received by the editor and is about to appear in print. The great thing is that I read, I think, I write, which I don't do in the course of my work. And it's all experience in a new field. Finally, I'm to write an article to commemorate your eightieth birthday. Hm.

All this happened because I know the editor, having met him in London. He's a gnomelike, thick-spectacled, cynically humorous man with at least an intellectual appreciation of my odd situation.

It's slow work enlarging one's acquaintanceship here. I'm so firmly based, by domicile, in the white camp. However, I'm on the brink of better things now, I think.

All the Europeans are nice, which makes their limitations more trying, but not one an aristocrat, in your special sense.[34] Or rather I've not met them.

I must confess I don't see much prospect of my job brightening. I suppose most of my reasons for going into business were specious, beyond wishing to be sent out here and be paid to come. My thinking now is that I shall certainly resign while I'm out here, at some time or other. It may be that I'm simply spoilt by King's, but I think that beyond that I'm not a commercial world person anyhow.

There is no room here for any human sympathy, none for one's fumbling efforts to give a hand to anybody. Alas no scope for any principles of any reputable sort. It is a second rate existence and I don't feel happy in it. The questions are when shall I break away and what shall I then do.

Locked Diary, 30 December 1958
The past year. What a lot has happened!

The deaths – E.K.B.'s on 13 June, Rose Macaulay's on [30 October].

The outings: Mediterranean Cruise with Bob and May in April, not as good as two years back, but good, and Venice charmèd, at the end.

Italy in Sept. with Tim Leggatt, good and not unemotional. He went off to Calcutta – P&O job – in October, and does not sound happy there.

Nick Furbank and the typing of 'An Unwritten Novel', which I wish to be preserved. Tim as aforesaid: earlier in the year I stayed with him and glided.

My deafness no longer distorts music and after trying hearing-aids I postponed their evil. But during the last few days it gets worse, and after my birthday parties (1, 2, and 9 January) I must do something.

Self confident and in good intellectual form during the month: broadcasts, interviews, photographers, journalism, well-bred assertions that I have had a happy life. Though have I? Or a miserable one? Certainly not an eventful one.

One thing that I very much enjoyed was the Bengali habit of 'adda', whereby, if someone calls on you unannounced, you share with them whatever suits the time of day – lunch or a drink or 'shondesh' (sweetmeats) – as against the English way of saying 'we're just about to have lunch, I'm afraid we don't have enough for an extra person'. In other words, you always share whatever you have, even if, strictly speaking, it's less than enough. That's generosity.

Commonplace Book, 31 December
Siegfried Sassoon

In byegone days I sometimes sauced a
Confederate croney – Morgan Forster
Query: do I now dare accost a
Figure as famed as E.M. Foster?
I do. In bed with glum lumbago
Watch I my words upon their way go,
And wafted by affectionate wings
Join the glad 'goings on' at King's

With Morgan I can still be 'matey'
Though grown so eminent at eighty.
I, ever so unintellectual,
And, as a thinker, ineffectual,
I, a believer in believing,
Can hail his genius for perceiving
Reasoned humanities which led
Where angels have not feared to tread,
And thus, forbearing further fuss,
Award my friend an Alpha Plus.

Lovely skilful sincere stuff and illustrating that 'I love you
though I never trouble to see you' attitude which is also
characteristic of Ben and Peter,[35] and which I do not share.

Morgan was eighty on 1 January.

Thanks to Morgan, in Calcutta I met Bishnu Dey, a prominent Bengali poet, translator and art critic, who won India's highest literary award, the Jnanpith Award, in 1971, and was a very distinguished scholar. In 1947, during the Hindu-Muslim conflict after Independence, Dey, a Hindu, in saving the life of a Muslim man, was injured in a way that affected the rest of his life. He was a close friend of Jamini Roy,[36] whom Morgan also knew and to whom he introduced me. I don't know how Morgan came to know him.

Indian Journal, 4 March
Bishnu took me to see Jamini Roy. He is a wonderful old man: bespectacled, bent, with quick, expressive hands, straight white hair, wrinkled, with a cigarette or paper on which he has jotted in his hand, some teeth missing, bright eyes, gentle, eager. He has experimented endlessly. He believes one test of a good painting is whether or not it will stand enlargement: he doesn't think realist painting can. He uses children's paintings, of which he has a great collection, and tapestry work – in fact primitive styles – for ideas.

Then, through my friends Brian and Cynthia I met the painter Paritosh Sen, a leading Indian artist and founder member of the Calcutta Group of painters, formed in 1943, that did much to introduce modernism into Indian art. I was fortunate enough to be given two of his paintings by him. Paritosh in turn introduced me to Satyajit Ray, one of the greatest film-makers of the twentieth century. He was amazingly talented – a writer of fiction, publisher, illustrator, graphic designer and music director. He first made his name with the three films of *The Apu Trilogy*, and altogether directed thirty-seven films. I was fortunate enough to accompany him while he shot *Jalshaghar* (The Music Room) and made the music for *Apur Sansar*.

I also met the great photographer Sunil Janah. Hence, I was able to enter a cultured Bengali society, from which I greatly benefited, and which of course further distanced me from conventional white society.

Commonplace Book,
Birthday good wishes
Wystan Auden's wish to me, 11 January 1959 (I read it at the lunch):

'Dear Morgan wish I could be with you in more than spirit stop may you long continue what you already are stop old famous loved yet not a sacred cow stop love and gratitude Wystan Auden'

EMF to TWL, 19 January
I have had three birthdays – the big one on the ninth here. All went well; at the big one 100 people, and no high table, which worked out excellently. I really enjoyed it very much, fed as usual, and not too tired. The stars were the two actor-boys from America, George Savidis from Athens, and Charles Mauron[37] (blind) and wife from Provence. And in terms not wholly of snobbery must be listed the Greek ambassador for he gave a most lovely silver coin of Demetrius Soter. All old Bloomsbury mustered, some of Fleet Street, and four cousins. Stephen Spender heard of what was afoot and sent heartfelt greetings.

Really the brightest piece of news in your letter was the journalistic. If you read, read, and review a little it is something and will keep you out of the morass of Acceptance into which it must be so easy to slip. People who know you better than I do have wondered at your accepting that job, and all the serious part of your letter makes depressing reading. What I feel about you is that besides holding the sorts of values I like, you are practical and likely to fall on your feet.

So I shouldn't be concerned about your breaking loose as I should in the case of some people.

Of King's:

Ah yes Tim what a good place this is – a place for the very old and the very young, I should think.

I wrote a piece for *The Hindustan Standard* in celebration of Morgan's birthday. In it, I wrongly reported his response to an American lady who asked why the Queen had inducted him in to the Order of the Companions Honour – which is stated to be 'in the personal gift of the Sovereign'.

EMF to TWL, 21 January
Of Bishnu Dey

I knew and liked him in 1945. He was <u>then</u> young sensitive charming, literary (T.S. Eliot) and art critic of merit, friend of Jamini Roy and other painters of the so-called Calcutta School and possessor of a fascinating collection of Bengali village toys. Left wingish.

We corresponded a little, then fell off, but this year I get a most friendly New Year Card from him and his family – same family I think, same address, anyhow.

I am writing to him by this post, telling him only your name and approximate age, and saying that if your business brings you Calcutta, you may be getting into touch with him, and could give him recent news about me. This leaves you free to write to him or not.

At this point I had more or less decided to resign from my job.

EMF to TWL, February
Fortunately you are still unmarried and can take risks. On the other hand the right private life for you is marriage plus children so I hope you will tumble into something that is sound economically before too long. Meanwhile a little journalism is all to the good.

I am writing from Aldeburgh, Ben's new house. I don't like it much, I have a cold and it is so cold, my only warm hour has been at Billy Burrell's,[38] burning driftwood that he has picked up on the beach. I haven't much news – the whole of this island has been more or less off colour and under fog.

Curious to think I may see the Brutus before you do. It is certainly a wonderful object.

EMF to TWL, 7 March
Your photograph, whether informal, semi-formal or formal, seems to have got framed on its way here. Wittily put, but when shall I receive it? I should like to. Also what you wrote about me. Also I have never heard from Bishnu Dey. Nor perhaps have you.

I am at last really of age – celebrations ended last Sunday with a loud and splendid concert in the hall offered me by the KCMS.[39] I was very pleased, and found no difficulty in making a speech – it is well for all concerned that I did not develop this gift earlier.

Today I doddled along to the Union Gramophone Room to an 'informal reception' by Mrs Pandit.[40] She was charming and gracious as usual, and longed, oh how she did long, to escape from official and diplomatic life. My other festivity has been the Ten Dinner in the Audit Room, an excellent meal and wine of which I must have drunk more than usual as I got very argumentative and gay and kept interrupting my two neighbours, one American and one Irish, when they tried to quarrel across.

All this must read rather trivial and rather sad when read several thousand miles away.

I add a very sad piece of news which I know you will be very sorry to hear. Pigou died this afternoon. He has been in Addenbrooke's [hospital] for several weeks, having no pain, but getting weaker and weaker, just fading away under old age.

TWL, Indian Journal, 19 March

Bishnu says that Morgan came to India with the approach of the modern anthropologist plus his extreme sensitivity but it was not enough for a complete understanding; hence the failure of Godbole,[41] whereas the simpler Muslims are well drawn. He only saw a section of India.

13 April

At Konarak[42] I found a tremendous pile of a temple set apart from man, by the sea: the old river beside it dried up, the old town long since vanished. And the temple being worn away by sun and salty wind, slowly decaying handiwork of man, though a monument to man's inspiration. What scores of erotic figures! They are teeming on its every side: frank, detailed, orthodox and perverted, innumerable: exuding a jubilation in the body, nature, life that was evidently irrepressible. Not man and wife any of them, just cavorting, caressing, petting, copulating men and women.

The bottom frieze is of an endless series of round-bodied chubby elephants. High on the walls are the twining tender lovers. Above, upon the parapets stand and play the big-breasted, barrel-thighed female musicians. The chariot is solid: could never fly, but would surely trundle.

On 15 April Morgan retorted to my January letter:

You muffled and muffed my retort to the American lady. I didn't say 'Because she liked me' but 'Because I told her to'.

Here's a little journalism from me, hearing you had been to Konarak. I wish I had, though as regards style I believe Khajraho[43] is better. Your letter was most interesting and redolent of the smell of burning boats. I have heard from Bishnu too, and am happy and proud to have been the means of introducing you to each other.

Yes I am likely to see Brutus, for May <u>will</u> go to Florence, and San Vitale for Bob <u>will</u> go to Ravenna, and Rome because both of them insist on going there. I am not quite in the travelling mood yet, and I shall have to talk the Italian from which you saved me. Please give Bishnu my love and I will write to him, and my most kind remembrances to Jamini Roy.

I resigned my job after six months, in April, and went to live with Bengali friends.

TWL, Indian Journal, 1 May

I once went out of Calcutta with friends to see a sunset. It was a perfect moment. Behind and above a splayed pattern of trees against the sky, in front a still meadowland. To one side clumped trees' bulky shadows, on another a few sharp-edged trees against the sun: muted colours. All about the throb of cicadas. In the distance the ringing voices of men far off. And the whole breathing evening was sinking imperceptibly and confidently like a giant tent. Against the order and inevitability, zany bats with impish random flight made arbitrary patterns, but could not, perhaps would not, disturb the peace. A small train, a harmless out of breath animal, puffed on its tracks across the twilight simmer and vanished away without a single whiff of smoke or breathless echo left behind.

EMF to TWL, 3 June

I hope another letter will arrive from you soon and give more of your plans. I always remember the admiration you once expressed for what may be called 'Australian strength' and wonder how this will combine with other admirations which you and I share, and how all will combine to dictate a decision. I am not the least frightened for you. At your age you still have plenty of time to peep and peck about, and to experience and experiment. I am so delighted that you are getting something out of India. I wrote to Bishnu the other day.

Here things are delightful on the surface, which is mostly composed of undergraduates and has offered me a most pleasant time. Deeper down – or rather higher up – I should call things interesting rather than delightful. Noel is well under way – active, ambitious, ambivalent – and some of the frogs are beginning to think they may have elected King Eel. I foresee a good deal of comedy ahead and perhaps some discomfort. He follows the pattern of Maynard Keynes, who grew up in the obscurity and integrity of Bloomsbury, then moved into the greater world of power-politics and compromises and was accused by Clive Bell and his earlier friends of betraying them. I don't think there is any moral judgement to be made over this development in a pattern, but it happens not to please me aesthetically. Some think Noel won't stay long, others that he will wait until the Tower of Annan has arisen – for this do they term the King's Lane Redevelopment scheme – and has stamped his tenure of office upon College history.

Saw Garry the other day, but no opportunity for talk. I wish I knew him better.

TWL, Indian Journal, 18 June
Bishnu took me out one evening to see some Kali *pujas*[44] in a small village not far from here. We arrived at the road's end to find a small railway station with houses straggling from it and without any electric lighting: just lamps and lanterns. We walked out along a clotted mud track behind a guide. It was utterly dark. No moon. Hardly a shadow standing anywhere around. And yet somehow my impression was strong of *Pather Panchali*[45] type countryside, of muddy fields and clustered silent trees. As we walked we heard the throb of drums and the shouts of a surging excitement. We arrived.

In the centre of the village was an open space before a long elongated structure housing the flowered and painted goddess. There was much *shondesh* around waiting to be offered, and occasional mystified goats unaware of their fate. People gathered in anticipatory huddles, slowly more and more, becoming more and more expectant and bright-eyed. A few, too few, drummers were trying un-optimistically to catch a mood of ecstasy. But no. They were too young, or too inexperienced, or too few, or it was too early: and they were not drunk. We wandered, waited, drowsed to pass the hours: and I almost passed out with an epoch-making weariness. Then 'would the drummers show us their paces, a few rhythm runs and artistry?' They thrubbed and battered with their sticks, and in time began to smile as though they were getting warm in their treasure hunt for the earth's own beat and passion. While we, our eardrums waffled by the noise, smiled too in vague appreciation.

A further adjournment, until I suppose about 2 a.m., and then the real work of the night was to begin. There had previously been a ragged series of women either making vows or more often giving thanks to the goddess, showing their devotion by progressing from their homes to the temple by alternating three steps with total prostration. This was a most sincere and moving sight.

Often, I am told, the priest who is to carry out the sacrifice gets himself quite drunk before taking the axe in hand. He has to sever each goat's head with one blow, or the meat will not be made holy and his own family will suffer a curse for the misjudgement of his hand. And he had on this occasion seventy goats for the slaughter, and that meant seventy spoutings of dark goat blood. But this night he was not drunk.

I did not see the axe-blade strike the first goat, but I could see the rudimentary block, the four men holding down the goat upon its side, the children gathering close for the primeval thrill; and then the priest's blank face, the gleam of the axe-swing, and I heard the quickening drums and the shouts of ecstasy and I felt the ripple of the crowd: then they rushed forward with the severed body, jubilantly flicking bloody baptisms upon the jostling faces, and flung it on the ground before the goddess. And if the body twitched in death the boys would smack it still.

A short time was enough and I went back and slept. And we trod the same path back to the car in the dawn, when the drumming and the shouting was over and All-India Radio or perhaps gramophone records had been substituted. In a way it was very unpleasant and even frightening. And yet not all that much. After all the goat died swiftly and its previous fear was not so very much protracted. If there was sadism, it was an honest purging, and its object was devotional. And clearly there was great, intense sincerity amongst many. And if their religion is so far violent, what is that? To each man his own belief, if it is not destructive. And why, and in what name, deprive the less sincere of their annual excursion and thrill? Some form of sacrifice is at the base of most religions and of many distinguished human achievements: the more sophisticated forms are not necessarily the more appetising and acceptable.

Tim Leggatt in Calcutta, 1959.

And yet, and yet to me it is an ugly thing that any man's god should call for so much blood – as many as seventy goats – and have to be appeased and titillated in that way. And I prefer that each man's drunkenness should be his own and not a public orgasm. If I am told that men attribute to their gods the desires that they fear to admit to be their own and which need to be expressed, and isn't this a comparatively harmless way?, well, I am interested but still I hope they will quickly find some other gentler dissipation or sublimation, so that they run away like rivers in the sand and the instincts of the mob are not aroused.

I was not offended by this spectacle. I was interested. But I didn't very much enjoy it.

EMF to TWL, 7 July
In Italy with Bob & May

Our big social success was at Cécina Marina, a small bathing-place south of Leghorn. I was sent into a working class café to enquire for rooms, and the owners not only took us in but took us to their hearts, and we ended in eating with the family. One of them studies English at the University of Pisa. This meant additional ease and an extra link. Such kindness and gaiety. But oh the noise at night, not so much the drunks as the communists. And by day there was Serafina, a refined looking child of three, who rent the welkin. I wonder where else one would find such generosity and warmth. Certainly not in France. Perhaps in India. When we left the bill was too small and bottles of beer and minerals were thrust into the car. Both Bob and I have heard from the Pisa student since our return, and I have given him the new Italian translation of *Howards End*.

Cécina made a profound difference to our tour, and seemed as it were to illuminate the scenery and art-objects from within. I certainly enjoyed myself very much on the whole, and did not take the inevitable interludes of apprehension and despair too seriously.

The college is empty, indeed completely so today for it is the staff holiday – Mrs Blackwell, Miss Perrin and the rest of them starting off at 7.30 for Windsor Castle, Hampton Court, and the Palladium. No one seems much pleased – too much walking say some, too much driving say others, and no restaurant in London has been found to accommodate the whole 117 of them, so they will have to dine in the Victoria Coach House. I have slept part of the day in the Fellows' Garden, all alone and my nearest approach to sun-bathing. The weather is torrid.

In due course I obtained a job as a lecturer in international relations at Jadavpur University in South Calcutta.

TWL to EMF, 20 July
No, no, it's entirely my fault, this failure to send a letter to await your return from the Pensione Belletini. But for the best-intentioned of reasons. I badly wanted to give you some definite news as to my future, and each week it seemed that I would know, so I put off writing. At last I know something.

I have been offered the job of lecturer in international relations at a small university on the south edge of Calcutta, called Jadavpur University. I have been told this unofficially so far. When I receive the letter of appointment from the governing body, I shall write to Noel and Arthur,[46] thanks to whose testimonials the offer has been made. But till then please tell them that I've been successful and that I'm taking the job for a year.

The subject is perhaps rather alarming, but the point is that it's a means to an end. If, after leaving P&O, my prime object was to survey anew, and more thoroughly, the whole field of jobs available to me, then, after some cursory touring, I would come speeding home. But that's not so. I feel it would be foolish just as soon as I'm beginning to have something of the feel of India to go home. I should always regret it. I've just made friends, and felt the stimulus of Calcutta. And what, at twenty-five, is one year spent in this way? I shall have sufficient pay to live on, good holidays in which to travel, leisure in which to read, further stimulus from Bishnu Dey, Jamini Roy and others, experience of teaching which could be my best metier. I realise that it could be said that I'm putting off the difficulty of further choice of a career (but I don't want to keep on stumbling and fumbling at this) and that I'm prolonging my university life (but why not?).

I hope that my decision appeals to you – though it does postpone my next visit to King's – and that it strengthens what confidence you have in me. Please give me your candid reactions. It may be that I've omitted certain steps in my thinking up to this present conclusion; but I'll always try to supply these later.

The new address, which please note tiresome as it is, tells you that I'm now living with a Bengali family. I only eat Bengali food, and am slowly learning the language. The Ts have two children [aged] seven and one. I have nowhere made better friends and love them both very much. We all three look forward to me staying on, till I leave, in their flat. So now I have a home, with all the security that suggests. And instead of being isolated and purely self-reliant, I have the touchstone of friends who share my ideas. I'm writing enthusiastically because, well, because I'm very enthusiastic. I feel so relieved so free and relieved to have thrown off the business clutch in which I was sure to be unhappy. I seem, possibly by illusion – but what a pleasant and refreshing one – to have rediscovered a vitality and spontaneity which I haven't had since pre-adolescence. Well, you can see that I am very happy now. So perhaps I shall make something of this year.

At this moment I'm in Bombay, travelling by train in third class,[47] where your last letter followed me, having put in visits to Ajanta and Ellora[48] before I start my new work in August. The caves and sculptures were all stupendous, but it was the Ajanta paintings which made my eyes shine: I thought they were exquisite. This venture is all that I can set against your Italy. Ravenna and Florence have a very nostalgic sound and remind me of the things I care for most in Europe. And your bit of real Italian life at Cecina Marina is wholly enviable. Even when roguish, as at the station restaurant at Piacenza, I love the Italians and would so much like to live in Italy for some worthwhile length of time. I am so pleased your trip was such an evident success, and for Bob & May as well as for yourself. I assume that your luxurious way of travelling made it quite restful: no suitcase heaving and so on.

I am amused by the picture you give of the swelling Noel trumpeting over the Cambridge campus. Francis[49] must be rather upset by the way things are going – with Jaffe[50] and the Establishment. Do you see Francis nowadays, as I assume he lives in London?

Having now some certainty at least about the immediate future I shall adopt a new letter-writing routine. I shall try to keep you posted more regularly. Unlike everyone else I ever write to, you know this country, and so I don't need to make the superhuman and ineffectual effort to convey the background of my life. I shall try to describe to you next time some of the people I'm meeting and mixing with, and the ideas that are going around. Bishnu of course I'm seeing steadily. I hope you are keeping well.

TWL, Indian Journal, 24 July
I visited the caves at Ajanta and Ellora. The countryside around this area is lovely, fairly highly cultivated, squared into green and brown fields, stubbled over with bushy trees, and totally flat for the most part. I came upon the Ellora caves from above, over the ridge. The plain was flat and in the centre was a gleaming lake: life stirred gently all over, birds, cattle, goats, occasional people on foot, on bullock-carts, in cars. The low ridge curved, slightly sheltering the thirty and more caves cut clean from its breast. These were monumental. Some of course rudimentary, but others fully worked and more or less elaborate. The Buddhist were impressive for simply cut vaulting and hardly varying iconography. Here is what the West thinks of as the inscrutability of the Eastern religions – row upon row of impassive Buddha-figures dominated by one gigantic solitary. The Brahmanical caves were more elaborate. Of these the masterpiece is the Kailasa temple, teeming with sculptural imagery: alas that I'm so unversed in the iconography. The last few are Jain, one of them especially delicate. Overall the impact of colossal endeavour is overwhelming. In time one takes for granted the habit, as it seems, of cutting temples and sculptures from solid rock: it's made to appear so easy. The fineness of the carving is able to express the sublime emotions of the gods

with remarkable consistency. Yet I did feel that there was missing the lightness and sheer joy of Konarak.

I also approached Ajanta on foot. This time beginning from the plain I walked towards a convergence of gently folding slopes, covered, if not thickly, with greenery. And, as I drew near, the way led on from the first inviting recess to another, curved to a third, and to a fourth: then the bosom of the enchanted hills lay bare and I could see above me the caves snuggling together and vanishing from sight round a further, it was the last, crook in the hillside.

Again some caves were incomplete and half-hewn while others were fully worked. The rock seemed softer than at Ellora, more porous I suppose. All caves were Buddhist. I was the first visitor and kept throwing open the gates for the first time that day, letting in the sun to reveal the great figures of the Buddha. But the paintings, existing if not well preserved in four of the caves, were a feast for a pilgrim. The colours are rich and deep and gradual: the lines economic and fine and delicate: the grouping and perspective is reminiscent of Christian medieval primitives, yet 1,000 years earlier: the subjects are secular and of infinite variety and naturalness. They were painted in the third and fourth centuries A.D. I think and were clearly the fruit of some great tradition of painting. I have never been made so joyful by any other paintings I have seen.

EMF to TWL, 28 July
Francis Haskell – all well, his fellowship renewed (three years). He continues to live here, and is in much better form than he has been for a couple of years. He is coming round in an hour with Robin Gandy and taking us to *The Three Sisters* – John Barton's last production before he moves

55

to Stratford. Norman also leaves, to teach mathematics at Eton. Kenneth has applied for a job in London – well paid and presumably commercial – and probably leaves too. All this is far from welcome to me, but since Francis Bennett died I don't set much store by Cambridge, am grateful to be here and that must be enough, and the Buckinghams still hold out, now three generations strong.[51]

I am having my sitting room done up – not in expectation of immortality but because the older I get the fresher around me I like things to appear. I am not sure that they will appear very well. The wallpapers are wretched.

It is so extraordinary having money when you are the person who is so unlikely to have any. I am determined this miracle shall be widely known

Locked Diary, 10 August
Jaffe and an evening walk
Dinner in Hall, excellent as usual but the menu already fades, and after dinner a donnish tiff with Michael Jaffe on the subject of *The Revenger's Tragedy*. I liked it, he didn't, and put into this harmless difference of opinion all his arrogance. Donnish tiff over, I took to the open air with Carlos van Hasselt[52] and we walked through darkness and decent drizzle up and down, while dozens of ducks walked over the lawn. It was a holy evening, until leaning over the bridge to watch the quiet river we saw floating down it: dead fish, and I remembered what century we were placed in. Now past midnight. Rain.

EMF to TWL, 27 September
I have never got on with any Bengal people except Bishnu and Jamini Roy. So touchy, and assuming they are the whole

of India. I have liked Mahrattas better. I hadn't heard of the comparison between the Bs and the French. The French are harder, aren't they.

I do go to Italy in about a month unless something goes wrong. One lecture only, entitled *Three Countries*, and only in two places, Rome and Milan.

I keep well and have just had my room done up – wallpaper much disapproved of by Kenneth ('well if you <u>want</u> your pictures to peep out of a jungle') and by Michael, who gave me an uninvited trouncing; but liked by me. Sort of underwater weeds occasionally puzzled by gold. Crimson cotton brocade curtains.

You are absolutely right not to wear Indian dress. One doesn't want to go native or go anything.

EMF to TWL, 20 October

The chief excitement – if I except the visit of Churchill – is the decoration of the dons' combination-room by Michael Jaffe which he did with great skill and the foulest of tempers. Scars are widely compared. He is better now, everyone likes the result, with the odd exception of Noel, who can't help feeling there ought to have been a west end decorator.

You will know that Garry has got a fellowship at Trinity. I must go and see him. I am not frightened of Garry.

This place is a bit sad with Norman and John Barton gone and Kenneth going. Why the hell does mediocrity quietly, inexorably, win?

Unfortunately, during the summer I had fallen in love with a married Indian lady. This reached a crisis point in October, and I decided that I couldn't live in India without her and so I would return to the UK.

TWL to EMF, 21 October

I am at present staying with Bishnu and his family in a tiny isolated village, just inside Bihar. The country is flat but immensely varied in colour, and the sky is huge.

I mean here to make up for my recent dismal failure to write to you. I shall start by going at length into what are at present the controlling happenings in my life, which partly explain my lack of letters. I have already written to my father on this subject. I now write to you as the only other person to whom I wish to talk.

It is not a request for advice, but of course I should be very happy if you will write to me about such critical matters.

I have got into a complicated situation here with an Indian family that consists of two parents and two children. As I now realise, the parents have been drifting away from each other for more than a year.

Rajiv had a hard childhood with a gentle weak father but a mother who was a woman of strong character, of tremendous self-will, formidably domineering and possessive. When he was small, his mother took a lover and separated from his father. The lover was a dipsomaniac and died of drink when Rajiv was twenty. Naturally she, and therefore Rajiv, was ostracised. For years he had no friends, and his mother kept him jealously to herself – not allowing him to see his father and intercepting any letters he received from him. Undoubtedly she loved him, but with what cruel selfishness!

He was forced to get a job where social background wasn't noticed. He did well. He is very thorough and painstaking and knowledgeable and competent where his work is concerned. In 1950 he got married and continued to live with his mother. In 1958 his mother died.

I myself believe that his mother made his life incredibly hard for him, much as he loved her. He was lonely, ashamed, driven into himself. He therefore became cold, very controlled, finding it impossible to commit himself, mistrustful of the world, unable to give himself.

His wife, Champa, is in complete contrast. She has always been highly impetuous, spontaneous, forceful and clear in her reactions. She was given a terrible time by her mother-in-law until, finally, she refused to continue living in the same house – a break which must have given her husband much pain.

They were never, I understand, especially close to each other. He did not much share with her. He concentrated on his work. Ultimately perhaps a year ago, she began to find him more and more moody, frighteningly reticent, evidently more attentive to the children than to her. While he felt that she did not love him so much any more. They neither of them spoke their feelings. And perhaps everything would have found a level in time.

But for me. I should say that I think I have changed. When I threw off my job, I became as free as a man can be of all compulsions. I became alive, gay, spontaneous, full of energy and confidence. And like this I burst upon them. My impression had been that they were very happy together, but now in retrospect I really think they were both reacting to me. I seemed to her more alive and varied than any of her friends: to him full of ideals, energy and self-confidence. So we became fast friends. I liked them both. I flourished, and talked, and became quite intimate with them.

Then at the end of July I found that I had fallen in love with the wife. I wrote to my father about it, who said 'then you should move'. But I didn't foresee what would happen, so I didn't move. I didn't appreciate that the marriage was limping.

What now seems to have been inevitable happened. The wife fell in love with me. And in September we wondered what to do. You cannot become the lover of the wife of a man who is your friend. There was no future for us. And yet I couldn't tear myself away; and she wanted me to stay – till I left India for good. It was of course very explosive.

Naturally I opened the crack in the marriage. Undoubtedly she felt closer to me than to anyone else, and loved me more than she ever had anyone. She realised that she had been losing her love for her husband. He found her less interested in him.

Then came two weeks' holiday with them in Darjeeling from which I returned on the seventeenth. There matters developed precipitately. I decided that the situation could not continue. I said to the wife that if I could not marry her, then I must leave her. I couldn't continue with the way things were. And nothing was to be gained by waiting. As it happened, on the very evening of the day on which I said this, he presented her with an ultimatum. He said: 'I know you don't love me. You must now decide whether you wish to make do with a marriage without love for the children's sake, or whether you wish to separate.' At this moment he is still in Darjeeling taking an extra week's leave; I am at Rikhia with Bishnu; and she is back in Calcutta, as she is a teacher. She is supposed to be making up her mind as to how she will answer the ultimatum.

But, whatever happens, I shall leave. Furthermore, I have decided to leave India and come home. I feel I must put distance between us: I cannot continue in Calcutta. I know this means resigning from another job, and I don't want the reputation of a resigner, but I just couldn't bear to live on here. I think it would be utter folly to stay on merely to show guts, or anything similar. And because I feel so lost, I think I must go home.

That is the whole story to date. When I return to Calcutta I shall tell you what she has decided. She is more like a domesticated Stephen Wonham than a Rickie;[53] it is therefore in doubt as to what she'll decide to be claimed by.

The events are catastrophic to all three of us. But like most catastrophes, I suppose they are quite normal. I suppose that most marriages that go somewhat wrong do so in this way. The fissure is made more apparent by a third party, and then perhaps worsened and deepened and widened. And next comes the time of discussion: patch up or separate. But this is little consolation. I realise that if I had taken my father's advice a great deal of pain and discomfiture would have been avoided. It is somewhat as though I had been carrying out an experiment with living people. Yet I could not withdraw. Some deeper, instinctive, possibly purely selfish, compulsion led me on. I do not yet know to what end.

I cannot say any more about it now.

I have slept on what I have so far written. I realise that what the last passage means is this. I have no conscience about what I have done. Of course I am anxious to avoid causing pain. But I feel that everything has been inevitable. I have not offended against nature. I know that I am the greatest thing in her life, and I refuse to admit that the greatest thing should be consciously denied.

If I come home I shall be making a fresh start in all ways. I shall come home, I hope having imbibed something of India. I have not seen a great deal: I have not met very many people. But I have been sympathetic, and have found the country congenial. I have the foundations for understanding. Beneath all the oddities and ritual, I have glimpsed India's wisdom, and how it reveals the shortcomings of the West. I am more tolerant, and perhaps more intolerant of intolerance.

I am drifting. I don't know what to do. I have always put people before all else, and wished to devote my energies to them rather than to any work. I have for a long time, perhaps irrationally, felt that I should have to be married before doing anything profitable. I wanted to give myself to another person in order to achieve the security and strength and confidence to go on to other things. Champa has confirmed this belief. With her I feel all my latent potentialities becoming actual. For her I could rise to unpremeditated heights.

I hope you will feel that this sharing with you is the product of love and confidence in your wisdom. I have in fact written far more than I did to my father, to whom I merely said that I think I must go home.

I cannot now start on the long-promised thumbnail sketches. Especially as I expect to be home within quite a short time.

Rikhia, where I now am, is a very spread out village: clusters of houses joined together only by a name. It is completely isolated. It is six miles to the railway station by a road which no car can follow. We have had two violent thunderstorms in the last twenty-four hours, and it is still raining. The ground is rocky and unfruitful.

Just a few lean cows and goats pass by herded by small boys with tattered umbrellas.

It is the perfect place for rest. I feel I haven't slept for seven months, and that I haven't rested for twelve years –

every holiday I have travelled. Also it is a place for reflection. So I am resting and reflecting all the time. Often rather aimlessly, but I have, as you now know, a fair amount on my mind.

I was most pleased to have your last letter. Perhaps, you will now be in Italy, or else you are just about to go. Whichever, it will be very good to have more news of you. Even when I do not write I think of you a great deal.

It was exceptionally important to me that Morgan received my three letters, but sadly he was away in Italy, so that they only reached him in Rome, where he was fully occupied with his British Council trip.

In Calcutta matters blew up, and I had to leave the flat I was living in. As I did so, Rajiv gave me a copy of Rilke's *Duino Elegies*, the gift of a genuine friend. Bishnu advised me against being melodramatic, but being young and in a very emotional state, I was. I felt that I had to leave not only Calcutta – but also India.

I returned to England in mid-November uncertain whether C would follow me, though this seemed unlikely on account of the children. I did meet Morgan for a number of talks, but I think we spoke principally about the future. I set about looking for more work that would take me overseas again.

I still didn't want to live in England where, I felt, so many disagreeable assumptions were made about Old Etonians.

Locked Diary, 29 December
End of year thoughts
Since, all being well, I go to Coventry tomorrow and see in the New Year there, and since I want to keep my luggage light. Most important events: birthday lunch stood me

by the College on 9 January: friendliness with Lindsay Heather:[54] Bob's illness, my second Italian visit. – these two in November. The death of Aunt Nellie[55] and the first Italian visit already noted.

Just back from Aldeburgh. Ben's. One night at Bill's.

C decided to stay in India with her family. About a year later I heard from R that C's father had died and she was quite heartbroken. Would I write to comfort her? I did so, and in this way restarted continuing close contact with the family. When she died many years later, he wrote to me, 'you'll never know how much she loved you'.

I was absolutely distraught, but Morgan took a different view.

EMF to TWL, 12 January
I am much relieved. I believe, and with reason, in love, but its initial stage can't last and if the subsequent stages have great practical problems to face there may be trouble.

Somehow or other Morgan and I found great difficulty in meeting.

EMF to TWL, 7 April
I had been thinking that we aren't seeing nearly enough of each other to please me, and that you would soon suddenly vanish. Well why did I not write? Well now I do write.

EMF to Ruth Cohen, Principal of Newnham College, 10 April
Refusal to deliver the Henry Sidgwick lecture at Newnham
I cannot talk seriously about the world today – which is what I would like to do – without coming to conclusions that are both depressing and unhelpful. Thanks partly to technical discoveries, all the things I care for are on the decline. The arts – especially the art of Letters – are weakening, the countryside is being destroyed, personal contacts are being

impaired, and we witness instead the triumph – by shock-methods of advertisement and psychological attacks – of what used to be called Mammon and is now called British Trade.

TWL to EMF, 22 May

I get very great pleasure out of all our meetings: in fact just to be with you is a pleasure. And, although we do not see each other as frequently as I should like, still our meetings are a vital part of my life.

Perhaps I am too introspective, but if I am, well, that is just a fact about me and gives me no shame. Anyhow, a graph of my mental ease, happiness, or what-have-you over the last six months would show it as starting low, sinking lower in January, and then in April setting into a further steady decline. I have now almost no interests in anything beyond one or two friends.

Possibly you sensed this. If not, you may wonder why I make this bald statement. I hardly know. But I do know that seeing you is something I look forward to, though I realise I have little to give myself. And somehow or other I wanted to bring you as close to the heart of myself as possible, and this seemed one way of doing it. It might help me and it's fairer to you.

I finally, following the suggestion of Tim Munby, a fellow of King's, found a job with Longmans, Green & Co., the educational publishers, as their representative in Ghana and Sierra Leone. I was to work a few months in London, and then go out to Ghana.

Commonplace Book, 20 July
Writing and death

Peacefulness to be found in writing. Why do I not write every day? Partly because I feel I ought to write well and know I can't. But that is not a good enough reason for not writing, if it gains me poise & peace.

Christians and Pantheists may insist that the soul is separate from the body, but this is not true. There is a live body, that is all.

When I went to west Africa, most of my work was in Ghana, which, formerly the Gold Coast, had recently become independent under Kwame Nkrumah. I lived in Accra, and tried to persuade the government to set Longmans books in primary schools. I also drove all over the country visiting secondary schools and bookshops, trying to sell educational books.

I drove to Cape Coast, where I knew a wonderful leper doctor, David Molesworth, with whom I used to stay, to Takoradi, Kumasi, Tamale, and even further North, to Ga.

I also visited Sierra Leone, the Gambia, Guinea and Senegal in the course of my book-selling work, and Nigeria for pleasure. I was in Nigeria on its Independence Day, 1 October 1960 – with the communist secretary of the Nigerian TUC!

EMF to TWL, 22 September

I am glad you like Accra, but wish you were more comfortably settled, and more in with Africans than you yet sound to be.

The Lady Chatterley case comes on some time in October, and Penguin says they will call me as a witness. I don't want this but it is one of those cases – they are not numerous – where one <u>has</u> to do one's duty. Prosecuting counsel will probably not be rude to me – I am too old for it to pay – and I am not, nor shall be worrying. It is to go before a jury, and I am full of admiration of the way in which solicitors have reduced my scattered evidential remarks into short brisk sentences which the jury will understand. Will they understand the book though? Many people have never read a book, only snippets or quarter-columns in the newspapers, and the appalling experience of three or four hundred long pages may bewilder them and make them unfavourable to liberty.

My play goes on and when it ends – which I suspect it may end soon – it is contracted to go on Broadway. So if all goes well and we visit Italy next year I should have plenty of money.

EMF to TWL, 26 October
I meant to write before but, though perfectly well have not been in good spirits, chiefly because young Rob (May and Bob's son) has been in hospital for weeks with jaundice and they have not discovered the cause; an 'exploratory' operation has ruled out cancer and stone but not cured him. This has diminished spirits and held up plans. Depressing too is the fate of Rooksnest (*Howards End*) which is likely to be built round in the New Town Stevenage expansion scheme. Its owners – my friends the Postons – are heart broken, indeed I think it will be the end of the old lady.

The college seems as usual, except that the under-graduates have become preternaturally polite. There was a small dance over my bedroom ceiling – profound apologies afterwards, guests got rather out of hand. There will be a small party under my sitting-room floor tomorrow – but only if I permit it.

The new fellows seem extremely nice. I have already mentioned Drummond Mathews who occupies Kenneth's rooms. The old ones go on all right, as far as my limited observations go. I get very little gossip.

On 20 October began the trial Regina v. Penguin Books Ltd., always known as 'The Trial of Lady Chatterley'. Morgan was called as a defence witness on 28 October, the third day of the trial, and testified to the book's literary merits. He was not cross-examined by the prosecuting counsel, Mervyn Griffith-Jones.

EMF to TWL, 30 November
Let me know when and if your travel plans develop, so that I may develop my character. I am very courageous about travel plans when they are distant and undefined.

I am having a very good time musically and write this between the first and the second hearings of Ben's Academic Cantata. But dreadful things go on outside one's little circle – e.g. the disappearance of the *News Chronicle*, already unlamented and forgotten by most. Advertising destroyed it and will destroy.

Papers can't pay unless they have advertisements: they don't get advertisements unless they can guarantee an enormous circulation; they can't get that unless they exclude distinction and decency. I see no way out of this trap. It is one of the unpleasant developments I wasn't prepared for. Another, for which I was <u>absolutely</u> unprepared is the rapid ruination of the countryside in all countries. I'm trying to stop worrying over it. The ruination of the human outlook through commercialisation is more serious (How to distinguish this from what I and others call legitimate enterprise I don't know).

Patrick has just become vice-provost – a very popular appointment. Everyone is pleased, even Sydney who is reported as saying that here is something worth suffering for. – Well that is the only scrap I can remember, so my mind evidently needs a rest. I spend Christmas as usual with the Buckinghams if everything goes well, or not worse. I may have mentioned that their son has been ill for some months. He seems on the mend at last.

EMF to TWL, 2 January

I write from Bob and May (Coventry) and have been here for about ten days, except for a couple of days at Rockingham.[56] But at Cambridge tomorrow. I don't get as much out of that place as I did, and it is not the place's fault. My general health keeps good, but that you will find me deafer blinder slower and perhaps fussier has to be feared.

Locked Diary, January 1961
The New Year

I spent the night of the 31st at Rockingham, and let the New Year in all alone and into loneliness, for no one inhabited the castle except myself and my host and hostess asleep far away in their separate beds. The moon threw its shadows – Norman, Elizabethan, Victorian – over the grass, to the left the elephants of the yew walk were visible (see *Bleak House*); ahead the little parapet with little balls and beyond it the vast mistiness of the Welland valley. One small light was visible in the mysterious expanse, one slight noise of clock or bell striking. The air blew past me into the castle, bringing what luck it can, and luck is certainly needed. I had no romantic thoughts. I had been sick earlier in the day, didn't want to have a chill and got back into bed where next morning Sir Michael Culme-Seymour Bt. R.N. brought my eighty-two years a cup of tea, followed by Lady Faith C-S with my breakfast. So the New Year dawned. Unusually.

Thoughts on the old year
Unlike the world in general I have had a good year:–

Play: Splendidly dramatised – started at Oxford in Jan, got to the Comedy Theatre in April and was only taken off last month. [57]

Lady Chatterley: gave evidence, was not cross-examined but hear I was one of the three witnesses who had most weight with the jury.

Sale of [Manuscript of *A Passage to India*] for £6,500 benefited London Library and is now super-housed in the University of Texas.

Portrait: Painted successfully by Colin Spencer.[58]

Private affairs sprawl less. I see that my friendship with Lindsay will not keep at the level where he started it. That lovely leather-case he had stamped for me in Milan, Sept 59 – no. He is all friendliness but used to me, and interested elsewhere.

EMF to TWL, 18 February 1961
Planning trip to Italy
I am afraid you may not find Italy lush:

non arva quae liris quieta
mordet aqua, taciturnus annis [59]

But it is easy to find a countryside that is not poverty-stricken and is picturesque. Let us cross and recross the side-spurs of the Apennines – leaving however all details until we meet.

Locked Diary, 2 March 1961
Brian Remnant

A look in before hall on Brian Remnant relieved and explained my depression: sex of the wrong sort, too literary and cerebral, weighs me down. As Brian was seeing me down the darkish stairs a lovely thing happened: the moon, just past full, rose at the opposite side of the court, first a pale yellow blur, then triangular, then round. I pointed it out, we watched it, he with his usual docility, and I asked him whether he ever felt that the earth was tipping down towards it, as it did then. He didn't seem to know. I said that it was lovely and that I was glad that we had seen it together, and nearly added that I liked him.

Ackerley, Joe, sentence in letter from: 'The days potter by here much the same; sometimes the sad sound of their ticking feet gets into my ears as they disappear into history, carrying nothing in their delicate hands but a yawn.'

Can the day that produced such a sentence be lost?

EMF to TWL, 7 April

I was in despair earlier this week, as I fell and fractured my wrist. It is still fractured but my fears that it would stop me from coming to Italy are groundless, the doctor assures me. Mercifully Bob was to hand in London, drove me back to Cambridge and after two days in the Evelyn[60] I'm just returned here. I shall see less than you will and sit longer than you expect to in a stationary Fiat, but that promises to be all, except of course a lot of help which I get anyway.

EMF to TWL, 16 April

Clouds threatened our holiday. They are not too threatening, and I believe all will be well. (i) The fractured wrist should be all right or, if not that, adequate – a bit of help in dressing may be needed still you'll give it. (ii) The slight heart-attack which now has me in Addenbrooke's should allow me to return to King's in two or three days and Leslie Cole[61] says that it need not return, and I may hope to accompany you.

Bob Buckingham to TWL, 30 April
I must tell you that Morgan was taken seriously ill again last Tuesday night and is now back again in Addenbrooke's. We were sent for and I really thought that on Wed evening he was at the end but he is now slowly improving and this morning is still better, but he is very weak and will be in hospital for some time yet.

EMF to TWL, 30 April
You will see that Italy is off. My wealth is enormous, part of the comfort of the present illness is having no worry whatsoever about finances. Going on to the stage has done it. I long to see you and have an affectionate and instructive talk. I can now be instructed on nearly everything, and I do earnestly want to know a little more about this gigantic item 'Africa'. I see Garry occasionally and much enjoy doing so.

TWL to EMF, 6 May:
I was most upset by your letter, and more at being so far away from you than at the collapse of our plans. I rather doubt that I shall go to Italy now, since the object was more to be with you and to re-capture and build on something of 1958 than merely to roam in Italy.

I shall not decide until I am back home. However, do not imagine that I am indecisive. I have already made the quite simple decision to come to Cambridge as soon as I can. I have chosen to return earlier than was previously planned. I have already written to Garry to alert him to find me a bed.

You will find that I have put on weight, and that I am quite heavily sun-tanned. Otherwise I am much as you remember and looking forward enormously to seeing you in less than two weeks... And especially to finding you in good spirits and to enjoying being with you again.

EMF to TWL, 18 May
Garry will tell you that I feel perfectly well, but weak. I don't know (and the doctors don't know) how long I stay here. I am interested to learn that you are larger and browner, and if this increases my pleasure in looking at you shall indulge it further. I much enjoyed seeing Garry.

EMF to TWL, 1 June
Not going to Italy, and with you, is being harder to bear than I expected. But I couldn't have met you next Tuesday even if doctors allowed as I'm uncertain over my feet: that big tumble I did back on Easter Monday has impaired their confidence. However it'll come back.

Write, and let me know your plans. It occurs to me before I close, to suggest – couldn't we, later in the season, hire a car and drive for two or three days in the west? (e.g. Hereford-shire, Welsh Marches) – I go to France in September.

Commonplace Book, 1961
A near-death experience
Nearly Dying, mid-June: meant to record this sooner.

No pain, no fear, no thoughts of eternity, infinity, fate, love, sin, humanity, or any of the usuals. Only weakness, and too weak to be aware of anything but weakness. 'I shan't be here if I get weaker than this' was the nearest approach to a thought. I know that Bob and May were to my right and left – they had been summoned by the police and arrived about 4 – and was not surprised and liked touching them: Bob's little finger pressed mine and pursued it when it shifted. This I shall never forget.

But this diverts me from the 'nearly-dying' moment that I am trying to recapture; for then I had no awareness of anything except weakness.

This experience has convinced me that death is nothing if one can approach it as such. I was just a tiny night-light, suffocated in its own wax, and on the point of expiring. I may feel differently when my death really succeeds, and others may feel different. I didn't find my mother different – she just stopped eating some nice stew which Agnes had made her and with which I was feeding her, and showed no perturbation although she had told me half an hour before that I should not have her long. And I find a close parallel to myself in the Caliph Amr, who conquered Egypt in the seventh century. A friend said to him:

'You have often remarked that you would like to find an intelligent man at the point of death and to ask him what his feelings were. Now I ask *you* that question.'

Amr replied:

'I feel as if the heaven lay close upon the earth, and I between the two, breathing through the eye of a needle.'

His experience was more colourful than mine, and he was aware of littleness whereas I was too weak to register anything but weakness. Still, there is a parallel here between two very different types of human being.

If a person had been present, imploring to be clung to, things might have hotted up, but I had fortunately remembered to give my religion as none or Humanist, and the sister must have put one or the other down. I feel now little hostility to the C. of E., for atavistic reasons, but can't accept either it or its more pretentious rivals, as a guide beyond death.

All this is written at Coventry, where I am convalescing – a convalescence not as complete as I hoped, for rheumatism has developed in my wrist, and a slight and occasional flutter and tightness round the heart. Disappointing, but disposing to serious thoughts. For it is serious to have had one's life 'practically' ending and then to be given a little bit more. I try not to hurry up and get another good deed or so in – a blunder which Lazarus fell into, I imagine – but the remembrance of that *almost* everlasting weakness and of Bob's finger seeking my own when I shifted is intensified, and I hope I shan't have a lot of pain during this addendum or cause a lot of extra trouble to those who love me and have brought me back.

TWL to EMF, 4 July
This will take you by surprise, that I am already back from Vienna. Garry and Tony Tanner[62] won't return until Thursday, but I flew back in advance. Not at all because I didn't enjoy the trip – indeed it was uniformly and thoroughly successful, but because I have had reason to change my July plans on account of a girl.

She is an Indian girl, from Bangalore, now in her fourth year in England, at LSE. I met her last year, but in the last month have with a precipitate rush got to know her intimately. I am attracted enough to want to see as much of her as I can during this summer. So I decided to cut short the Vienna visit, I think after the marrow had been extracted from it. I am going for a trip with this girl (whose name is Sanjita) to the West Country: which means that you and I need not go far west in August.

I said nothing to you of all this when we last met because it was only on that same evening that, on seeing her in London, things began to accelerate: then I discovered that she also wanted to see as much of me as possible. And so, because I've only just over six weeks left, it seemed foolish not to plan to do something together as soon as possible.

Although we have not reached it yet, either of us, it is nevertheless already clear that we might come to the point of wanting to get married. Obviously therefore it is terribly important not to rush headlong. You may perhaps think that we have already done this in planning to spend two weeks together. My mother and Andrew[63] both think so: that we are asking to be rushed into inextricable commitment to each other and into the feeling, which might in later circumstances turn out to be illusory, that marriage should be the next step. I do not think that this is necessarily so, and the fact that this view has been put to me should make me tend to wariness.

Inevitably, with this change of plans, I have hinted at my possible intentions to my parents: they had anyhow probed when I had S here for one weekend. Regrettably, we have had a rather agonising talk about hypothetical possibilities. The unfortunate thing is that my father is very colour conscious, he has a physical distaste for coloured people. So it is clear that, if ever I did marry a coloured girl, we could hardly be very happy in the atmosphere which would result at home. And so I suppose I should not see much of my parents. Certainly my father thinks this, which distresses my mother as much as me.

Naturally there are many other objections, the most important of which is the consideration of the lot of a half-caste child. Do you regard mixed marriages as doomed to great stresses and hurts? Do you think that people should do all in their power to avoid them? Personally I am not quite so pessimistic as all this, though I am most conscious of the great weight of responsibility involved in begetting children in a world so generally colour-conscious. The difficulties are surely not insurmountable even though great. They might, I quite see, lead to dictating where one lived and what walks of life and what societies one should eschew.

My father has just said that he feels certain that if S and I go off together the irrevocable step will have been taken. I wonder, perhaps I haven't considered carefully enough the implications of this plan. I wish I knew what you thought.

My true position is that I am not quite clear about my feelings and I want to sort them out. I cannot say exactly how intense they are. I want to know quickly because I am home for so short a time. I thought this was the simplest way to find out. Is this unthinking, naive? Would I be crossing imperceptibly and inevitably from involvement to commitment? I had not thought so, and I don't think that she had. Surely, surely not: I am sure I can name a great many instances where this kind of holiday has been undertaken in the same way. However, tomorrow I shall aim to discover what implications S sees in our planning – and perhaps think again in the light of these.

I do so wish that I could see and talk to you at a moment which may be so important to me. But there doesn't seem to be time. The best I can do is to bring you up to date and of course keep you closely in touch.

I hope all your news is good and that you can get about as much as you wish to without feeling tired.

EMF to TWL, 8 July

I have waited to write until the promised postal address arrived, and I won't go into the various problems raised by your letter – except to say that emotionally I am in full sympathy. (Had it been possible for me I would certainly have married or tried to marry an Indian or Egyptian girl.)

Here everything is saddened by Donald Beves'[64] death, and it was painful to entertain a lot of strangers, including the American ambassador, under a flag which flew half-mast high.

After my holiday with Sanjita in Cornwall, Morgan and I took a five-day holiday in July in the Cotswolds and Herefordshire, staying mainly in farmhouses. We always shared a room, which was convenient and agreeable.

The trip included the Coln Valley, Kilpeck, and Deerhurst. We looked at many Romanesque churches and the most complete Saxon one at Deerhurst.

The high point of the Cotswolds was the Coln Valley, with its lovely villages. At St Mary's in Fairford we enjoyed the exceedingly beautiful stained glass windows made c.1500. We also took in Quenington, Coln St Aldwyn and Bibury, with its seventeenth-century cottages, which William Morris called 'the most beautiful village in England'; and also Northleach.

Kilpeck church is described by Pevsner as 'one of the most perfect Norman village churches in England, small but extremely generously decorated, and also uncommonly well preserved'. We loved Kilpeck and also Abbey Dore, with its lovely church, once part of a Cistercian abbey. We ended our trip in Tewkesbury with its splendid Norman abbey.

EMF to TWL, 1 or 2 August
I am sure that you are right and that it is time you fixed up with a girl, but it is wretched that such difficulties should attend this one – the short time that you have known each other well, the short time in which you have to decide, and apart from both these the dreary social problems of race. The appearance of Alex[65] last night brought home to me the dreariness and unreality of this last one. Still there it is – interrupting human relationships when it gets the chance to do so.

What a marvellous five days we had. For me, one of the few events that help the past and the future as well as the present. Meaning of which is (i) I enjoyed it (ii) so much so that I no longer regret Italy (iii) and also look forward to France. The splendid weather, scenery, and buildings large and small combined with your kindness and affectionate care for me. I don't know when I've had such an outing. I wonder whether we shall repeat it. Not very likely. Still, eighteen months ahead are better than three years.

EMF to TWL, 8 August
I wonder what decision about marriage will be reached. My own opinion – a very tentative one – is 'no', an opinion so tentative that if you and she settle 'yes' I shall forget I ever held it.

EMF to TWL, 14 August
From Ben Britten's house
I have forgotten where you are, nor have I anything special to say. Still it is nice communicating while we are still in the

same country. Garry called on me before I left Cambridge, I was so very pleased to see him. I got here a day or two back, garden large and for the moment sunlighted. Sounds of musical composition proceed from Ben's elevated shed. Through the hedge is a bungalow estate, one of them inhabited by the Burrells with whom I sometimes stay; all seems to be well there too.

Really I have nothing to say, which, when one has said what is most necessary, is very natural.

EMF to TWL, 25 August
It is odd to be suddenly far away from you and I am thankful I said all I did. It was the only moment when it could be said. I should like further photographs – architectural ones, e.g. Kilpeck, Leominster, Abbey Dore and the tympanum we saw rather late on – I forget the church's name – the Christ in Glory giving, as that subject seldom does, the impression of power without disagreeableness. The widely parted legs helped.

All goes well personally. I am here trying to dodge Adcock[66] but with no greater threat in view. Kenneth has been around, cheerfully teasing him:

'Darius didn't reach Australia did he?'

A: 'For a period of thirty years – it is rather remarkable – the Achaeminid kings were unshaven, then they reverted to beards again.'

K.: 'Dollars gave out.'

All too slight when transcribed but gay when rushing past.

I suppose most outsiders would say 'no' to themselves, however tentatively, over the problem of S and yourself. So many practical difficulties – and it is so impossible to weigh affection against prudence. I believe that affection should win when it is deeply established, but I believe that it can only be deeply established with the assistance of time, and I was worried that you had to make a decision before you had had the opportunity of knowing each other under varying circumstances.

TWL to EMF, September

I did, especially in Cornwall, have so much happiness with her. By and large I am sure that it is best to let things lapse, despite the moments (such as now) when I feel miserable about it. I suppose that I shall simply let time take its course, as I have done before.

That, very briefly, is how things are now. Not too good. I alternate between accepting this outcome and not wanting to. Quite apart from my conclusions and convictions, I am deeply anxious about leaving S as I have had to do. It cannot be helped, in that I cannot not go. But I know very well that she will be very miserable.

I enclose for you the three photographs taken in Sylvia's[67] garden. I have had all my shots developed. Many of them are very good. Would you like me to send all that I think you'd want? Do you want, for example, photographs of Kilpeck?

I went last Monday to King's to see Noel. It came from a sudden impulse. I haven't been really content about my job, and so I thought I'd lose nothing by getting Noel's advice on any alternatives that might be open to me. He was most kind, sympathetic and concerned. However, nothing positive has immediately come of that talk.

In fact my present feeling is that I would probably do well to stick to Longmans, where there is a place being kept warm for me and where I know that I am wanted. I feel sure

I should not find myself so much valued anywhere else. I still feel glad though to have seen Noel.

Otherwise no news. I shall be back in Accra by the time you read this. I don't much look forward to it on account of being tired and feeling gloomy and uncertain about so many things. However, probably, when I get busy again and involved once more in Ghanaian affairs (which promise to be lively, Alex says) I shall feel better. I hope so.

I do hope that you found your Aldeburgh stay relaxing and peaceful. It sounded from your letter to be so.

Well, thank you for our memorable holiday and for all your support and affection. I am very pleased that you said all that you did when we parted at your flat. I shall always remember it. I was very inadequate: and still am. But I do feel confident of seeing you when I am next back. And I will be a better correspondent this time, I hope.

Best wishes for your trip to France and for your continued good health and spirits.

Forster in Silvia Buckingham's garden, early 1960s.

Here I returned to Ghana. I was quite disturbed by my experience with S and at the same time I was getting obsessed with the conviction that it was time I got married. I was nearly twenty-eight. I met an English headmistress of the right sort of age whom I thought I would ask to marry me, and then I, mercifully, scotched the idea. I was not, on reflection, of very sound mind.

And I didn't know if my future still lay with Longmans or elsewhere.

We returned from France on 19 September and your welcome letters arrived a day or two afterwards. It was a very good tour. I kept well, and my wrist, after which you kindly enquire, got stronger so that I eat less awkwardly. The Maurons had excellently installed us over a gay and local restaurant kept by an Italian which had quiet rooms behind. Delicious food, and here we stayed nine days, seeing our friends daily and getting to know their boys. Then by remote and recherché roads to Geneva to stay the night with Ted Gillott and his Swiss friends. There followed the big surprise – the Vosges. Bob's intuition took us to a tourist perch in which we were the only tourists, and I lay in bed watching the crescent moon sink into miles and myriads of trees. The weather throughout was perfect and he and May looked after me as you did in Herefordshire. I needn't say more and can't. Thence a long drive to Compiègne, where we stay at a hotel which can scarcely have altered since my father was there in 1874.

Now about you. Your life and work seemed all right at the time of your writing, but I gather that the congenial and independent side of the work will not last, and that ultimately a London office must either be faced or backed out of. You're still safe in your twenties, and, being neither a husband nor as far as I know a father, still pretty free. So a second move shouldn't be risky though I think a third one might be. Since you've got a decent commercial job you <u>must</u> move out of commerce, you'll never do better there. Like you I dislike it and this college has just experienced commerce at its most indecent; housed a conference of expense-accountants who not only never conferred, not only got drunk and shouted but were sick all over the place and broke a quantity of furniture. That's what middle-aged businessmen can do, and that's what happens to a college that is too keen on money. They are, however, not to come here again. So I'm against commerce more than ever – to the point of being snobby about it. Something salaried and administrative would be better for you, despite its tameness, and despite the probability that you would only get it by strings being pulled. I wonder whether Noel has suggested anything. I am sure that he wishes to be kind, though it is the only thing about him I'm sure of.

This letter nears its close without mention of S. But you and she both know that I think your joint decision a wise one.

EMF to TWL, 27 October
Ghosts
I like the photograph of us standing in Sylvia's garden and think of getting it enlarged.

Interesting visit from a Ghana boy brought by an English one from John's. He has an English name (mixed marriage) but looks all black and was brought up partly heathen. His mother (who nearly died) was not the least perturbed at the change, since she would of course remain near or in the house guarding it, and he himself, in Cambridge, still has great difficulty at <u>not</u> knocking at doors of empty rooms in order to acquaint the ghosts. He belongs to the Aken tribe, Fanti division, and lives at Cape Coast Castle. I hold that faith myself in a remote inoperative way. That is to say I can imagine myself guarding Rooksnest after my death or you perhaps Parsonage Farm[68] after yours, but as soon as one starts moving from flat to flat and as soon as society moves from the rural to the industrial – what is one left to guard?

I have also seen Nicky Kaldor[69] who brought pleasant and appreciative news of you and was interesting on Ghanaian generalities, but I had no sense of <u>privilege</u> talking to him as I had with this black boy – I use 'privilege' because it was what you used when we ate bacon sandwiches with those men and that dog in the pub.

My heart always goes out to those who are not interested in their personal death, and one of my complaints against Christianity is its emphasis on it and its cult of the Last Moment – a moment when the dier (dyer?) feels weak and is probably either scared or doped as well.

Forster and Tim Leggatt in Silvia Buckingham's garden, early 1960s.

As for your work, it sounds as if your colleagues have found out you don't like it, however loyally you do it. – I am not clear as to what new job you are being offered, and how it differs from your present one. Maybe I haven't been reading carefully enough. But let me know.

College news in order of importance is the arrival of the Rubens[70] in the chapel, the appointment of Angus[71] as university treasurer (necessitating the appointment of a new first bursar, evidently from outside) and the election of David Holbrook[72] to a roving sort of two-year fellowship. I don't know what to make of this last. He is obviously edgy and difficult, but Eric Fletcher,[73] who had to do with him in that Cambridgeshire College set-up, is against him on other grounds. Philip Noel Baker[74] has been made an honorary fellow, to the general approval.

My personal affairs go well. The *Passage* should open on Broadway early Feb, with Zia Mohyeddin[75] as Aziz, Eric Portman[76] as Fielding, and Gladys Cooper[77] (!) as Mrs Moore. Another American, Mrs Elizabeth Hart has made a good dramatisation of *Where Angels...* And I have personally written an introduction to some short stories of Lampedusa's[78] (who wrote *The Leopard*). So on and so forth. The bad news is the ill news of young Rob Buckingham – in and out of hospital with temperatures of 103 and they fail to diagnose. Undulant fever is a possibility. It is frightful for little Sylvia.

I go for Christmas to Rockingham, and then Bob fetches me to Coventry. I can't see beyond that, anyhow not beyond 22 January. That was my mother's birthday, and I have fallen into the habit of getting flowers for it into my room. Hardly anyone knows where her grave is, and I have ceased to mind myself, but there is a pleasant memorial to her in Abinger[79] Churchyard: the sundial which used to be in our garden.

Locked Diary, 31 December
1961 retrospect

Bad: May's eye. Bob's back
        My illness – April to May
        Rob's illness, October on.

Good: Tim and self to Herefordshire
        Bob May and self to France.

Locked Diary, 16 January
Rob Buckingham

The worst of all my Januaries, which is saying much. Young Rob is in the West Middlesex Hospital, dying of Hodgkin's disease. I have the appropriate reactions but don't get knocked out and this may be because I am old. It started with jaundice last year and he said with impatient splendour 'I will get well' and the will seemed to triumph but three months ago temperatures sent him to hospital. Brucellosis, a type of undulant fever, was expected and now comes this grave diagnosis.

He is weaker each time, and irritable though not with the chance visitor – I have just looked back in this book at the entry of his birth – 21 April 1933 – how this book has endured while flesh go to their graves. I wonder whether he will see this birthday, I fear so, for this particular death is said to be slow, and may be prolonged if we get specialist treatment. Little Clive, held up by his grandfather – my Bob – waves from the end of the ward.

I have nothing but praise for the hospital, Sylvia, May, and indeed for myself, for I haven't been demanding or lachrymose and am pouring out money. Bob is the earth mourning, dense to hints and then stunned: he and I will not be together in one sense any more. Ahead looms deprivation as well as trouble, for we 'seven', as May likes to put it, including the two noisy infants – were as I put it a symbiosis and had created a rhythm that worked perfectly, thanks largely to her. We shall scarcely get to Czechoslovakia in September, for Rob's perishing body must not be left in too much loneliness.

Sweet Rob, how did he catch this devil? And where, when the hospital turns them out can they go and await their conclusion?

I don't think there is anything devilish in these occurrences, though I have not the advantages of praying to God, so vaunted by and for Christians, but on the other hand I have not the disadvantage of wondering 'Why did God allow this?' which takes up so much Christian time. We seem to me to have to make the best of a non-recognising universe, which is neither friendly nor unfriendly. The idea that it plays tricks on us is fatuous.

Why I keep trying to knock sense into my life or into the lives of those I love I do not know. It seems to be part of the human build up and when humanity has been unbuilt it may no longer exist. And at the end of this useless thoughtful day I am glad to have got down what it is that we are thinking about and that we are vowed to the ephemeral cult of Love.

At this point I was sacked by Longmans when I decided not to accept the offer of a job in London. I did not want it, I was doing a useful job in Ghana, which I enjoyed, but to them it was significant promotion. 'Since you have decided to seek your future elsewhere, steps will be taken to replace you as soon as arrangements can be made.' I did in fact write a conciliatory letter in answer to this, but it crossed with another from the outraged overseas director giving precise details of my successor's arrival in Accra and my departure, ending 'thereafter you will leave the company's service'. So that was that.

EMF to TWL, 24 January
I am sorry you should again be thinking of changing your job. I would rather you had found what suits you, and a girl to

suit, and got established. I can understand their disappointment when you wished to think over an offer they considered irresistible, and can hear the word 'contumacious' being exchanged behind your back.

I wonder whether we shall go away together again. It doesn't look impossible from my side, since I shan't be going abroad this autumn with Bob and May. We had planned for Prague, but a most depressing blow has fallen: young Rob has been for three months in hospital with temperatures: undulant fever had been suspected. He has now responded to treatment, and comes home next Sunday and there is even talk of a return to work. But he is far from well, and his parents don't wish to leave England – indeed May's presence is imperative for she helps Sylvia weekly with housework and the children. I have known for twenty years that she is a marvel. I hadn't realised that Sylvia would prove to be another. I feel more and more involved with that family and with their troubles, which have been nearing the tragic.

Locked Diary, 26 February
Bob et al.
How few are left to be loved: Bob (likely soon to change greatly), May, Eric, Kenneth, others are moving away – Joe – or have long ago moved – H.O.M.[80] The frightening truth came to me in this cold college, which misses no one.

EMF to TWL, 6 April
I will begin my letter where your Sierra Leone[81] one left off – namely with the possibility of our meeting. I will keep the first ten days of August free, and we will meet as soon as possible after your arrival and see what can be done. Shall

we go to Ireland and hire a car to drive about in there? Anyhow there is something to think about. I should like a change from Cambridge and like it now indeed, but since my illness last year I feel less vigorous and competent for solitary travel. In September I ought to go to St Rémy with May and Bob, and make it a centre for the month: we all love the place and my great friend Charles Mauron lives there. But this is doubtful, and for a tragic reason: the illness of their son (his age now twenty-eight) is incurable and will kill him sooner or later. He is back again in hospital now.

My pleasantest news is that some family documents have been discovered, relating to my gt-gt uncle Robert Thornton,[82] who went to the bad in 1814. Hitherto I hadn't known what happened to him. I am now sorting them out, just the job for my present state.

I have also just seen *Beyond the Fringe* and had a word with Jonathan[83] afterwards. He seemed in excellent form, and like all four of them boundless in energy. Their show goes on and on – well so does my *Passage…* come to that, and on Broadway.

Locked Diary, 7 April
Rob; sex

To celebrate Bob's absence I have spent the day as unusually as possible and dined alone in my room on avocado pear, egg dish, viener schnitzel with two veg, an apple, and drank half a bottle of champagne to him and smoked a small cigar. Rob may be dead. But whether I know what has happened or not, it happens. That is my recent lesson.

Another lesson. It is always being pointed out – and rightly – that the anticipation of sex and love is more satisfactory than their fulfilment. But the <u>recollection</u> of them is also satisfactory, that gets forgotten.

14 April

The doomed Rob is back in his home. I found him there, just returned from hospital, when I called this morning. I don't know what he knows, he is very weak and wanted to drive me to Liverpool Street.

EMF to TWL, 30 April

I am just back from Weymouth where Rob was 'convalescing' from a recent bout, seemingly in perfect health and certainly in good spirits. Sylvia there, also Joe Ackerley. They had a car, the weather was perfect, first time for four months, we all enjoyed it very much while Bob or rather May looked after the children in Coventry.

The weather is back to bitter, sky dark grey, the clouds not moving in the eternally moving air.

EMF to TWL, 27 May

I wonder what you will think of the social and physical face of England when you see it. It doesn't cheer me. It is more and more the paradise of the expense-accounters and the psychological advertisers. [Illegible] rules by new methods which I can't follow or hope to outwit. Nothing for elementary education, nothing for the probation service, which was promised a twenty-five per cent rise, the countryside ruined. The above remarks may be merely appropriate to my age but I shall be interested to hear what remarks you make when you've had a look around. Big business gaining still bigger powers through secrecy – that is my nightmare… it's wonderful to think we're meeting soon.

Your suggestion of Italy instead of Ireland excites me much and I have a feeling, fallacious no doubt, that it might be easier to fix. (I have become immenslier rich since last week and can shoulder transport for us both without the least difficulty).

At this point I returned to the UK. I actually had a job to go to, at PEP (Political & Economic Planning[84]), working on a research project concerned with students in the UK from the three East African countries of Kenya, Uganda and Tanganyika: how they set about coming here and what were their experiences when once they arrived.

I had no background for this except that I knew a little about Africa – in the West, several thousand miles away.

Locked Diary, 25 July
I am shocked – only slightly of course – by George Trevelyan's church funeral, the last time I had any consecutive talk with him he said with detachment 'I am sorry Janet has gone but I am quite sure I shall never see her again.' ('I do not really want to,' I think he added, but cannot be sure.)

I miss the disappearance of my co-evals – e.g. Lord Sandwich.[85]

We now went to Italy again, flying out to Milan. Hiring a car, we went to Bergamo, Verona, Vicenza, then Padua and Mantua, before returning to Milan.

My principal memory of Bergamo is, after we had visited the Basilica of Santa Maria Maggiore and I had gone ahead down the steps outside the church, Morgan, following, tripping and stumbling down a good many steps before coming to a halt beside me and giving a small bow, with a modest smile on his face, in acknowledgement of this physical feat. Very typical of him: an achievement, gently performed, modestly celebrated.

I have several cultural memories. First, seeing a production of *Tosca* in the Arena at Verona, when every member of the audience was given a small candle so that the amphitheatre twinkled all round with these tiny lights – a magical effect. Second, in Vicenza the many buildings designed by Andrea Palladio, and especially the beautiful Teatro Olimpico (built 1580–5, the oldest enclosed theatre in the world), with its trompe-l'oeil onstage scenery. Third, the magnificent equestrian statue by Donatello of the Venetian general Gattamelata, in the piazza in front of the superb Basilica of Saint Antonio of Padua. And fourth, the courts, galleries and gardens of the Palazzo Ducale di Mantova.

TWL to EMF, August

What a good holiday we had! How much, more than ever, I have regretted leaving Italy and returning to England! I am so deeply pleased that this was thought about so well in advance, and that Ireland was discarded, and that all our arrangements went so well. And I must thank you for laying on the car, albeit driven (& scratched) by me, and for fixing the financial side of our travelling by air and road. Without which, of course, nothing would have been possible.

It was better, I thought, even than 1958; I can't explain why. Possibly our identity (sic) of trattoria and hotel tastes was even more established, or the car made a big difference. Perhaps both. Or perhaps the mere fact of having known each other four years longer. Anyhow, it was most happy and memorable for me, and I just hope we can repeat some or all of it again.

EMF to TWL, 13 August
Thank you Tim for doing all you had to do for me, and even more for doing all you did that you needn't have done. I am writing short notes on a few items we saw – missing out the jokes and ephemeral anxieties that are liable to impinge.

I found Rob back in hospital, recovering from fever and delirium, he was on the mend and may soon be out again. Except for such help as I can give, I don't like being in England – e.g. the podginess of the beds is so unattractive, ditto the braised beef.

EMF to TWL, 21 August
I do hope we manage something again. I did so like it, and I never felt heavy and tired during the day time, as I do here.

Did you see, in the *Guardian* of 12 August, that the scenery caught fire before the performance of *Un Ballo in Maschera* and 22,000 ticket holders watched the blaze?

EMF to TWL, 24 August
I have had a pleasant meeting with Tony Tanner here. He speaks with decency, warmth and sense about the universe, etc.

I have furthermore to inform you of a political decision. Greatly though I dread and dislike both the USA and the USSR, I feel disposed to support the former for the reason that it has experienced a nineteenth century.

Locked Diary, 8 September 1962
Rob

Rob died 7 p.m., a couple of hours after I left London.

I saw him soon after he was born, April 1933. I last saw him about a week ago; he was conscious, grateful, affectionate.

9 September

Beginning to know what has happened. In the Three Hills, Bartlow, of enchanting beauty, I could only think 'Rob has never seen this and now never will.' His lovely eyes will go to the hospital. I have found half a dozen of his letters to me. He was romping ahead but the disease caught him up, aged twenty-nine.

10 September

May was allowed to wash him not long before he died through the courtesy of the night nurse. She was with him when he died. I long to talk to her when she can bear it. I like what she says. I <u>think</u> life may run smooth again; but we all have shattered nerves and I behaved peremptorily in Hall, and I have knocked off alcohol the whole day as a whim.

9 October

Have made three resolutions, unfortunately simultaneously: to prepare the first section of *A Surrey Ramble*[86] for publication; to prepare *The Torque*[87] for non-publication; to prepare the Robert Thornton letters for reading at the Memoir Club.

On 14 October the Cuban Missile Crisis began when a United States Air Force reconnaissance plane discovered that the Soviet Union was building launch sites in Cuba for missiles which would have the ability to strike most of the continental United States.

EMF to TWL, 26 October

It was a special pleasure to get your letter. It has been followed by a visit from your aunt,[88] indeed she has just left. We talked away fine. I'm not unfortunately going to see her play, because of a sprained ankle. I much liked her visit and so admired her pleasure in acting some of the younger dramatists' stuff.

I think I'll finish now dear Tim. My last London visit was to see Joe Ackerley get the £1,000 W.H. Smith literary prize. My next to see you, I hope. I gather you could do with a prize too, prices are appalling.

My chief reading for the last three days has been *Hamlet*, attending for the first time in my life to the words, and discovering how very few of them I understood. At Coventry I went to a very good play called *The Bedmakers* by David Hunter, thought I had discovered him, wrote, and now find that he had already been discovered by L. Olivier, opposite whom, in his first play, your aunt should have played. Thus do things join up, not always perfectly.

On 28 October the Cuban Missile Crisis ended when President Kennedy and the UN Secretary General, U. Thant, agreed with Nikita Khrushchev, the Soviet leader, that the Soviet Union would dismantle its missiles in Cuba and return them to the Soviet Union; in exchange the US made a declaration that it would never invade Cuba and would dismantle major missile systems in Europe and Turkey. For two weeks the crisis was the haunting background to the everyday life of everyone in the country.

EMF to TWL, 4 November

It is much too long since we met, and after the Buckinghams you are the person whom I most want to get away and see. I have been held up by an ankle (sprained on Staircase B) and a toe (origin dubious). But all now seems much better. Sorry to be a bit tentative and vague. Let us try to hear the sound of each other's voices anyhow.

The photograph is a terrific success. How clever I was to ask you to take it, not to pursue the matter further. Thank you very much.

Many messages from Bob and May. Their reactions (and Sylvia's) to the disaster are as satisfactory as could be expected. We light a bonfire for the children Monday night.

Locked Diary, 8 November
Arthur Cole & Malcolm Darling

Arthur Cole,[89] the College's leading benefactor and bore, has come up for the Audit Feast. He is now deaf, but wouldn't attend to what one says if he could. My dislike of him is discreditable and such as an old man can only feel towards another ditto whom he has known for years. I date it from thirty years back when he refused to let his best friend (Malcolm) marry his daughter. He did it so coldly and primly, all his past protestations of affection vanishing. The girl seemed right for Malcolm and might have brought him much middle aged happiness. M – who is also up for Audit Feast – will have put this far away in the generous depths of his mind.

25 December

More Christian thoughts than usual, written in bed after a suitable day. Thinking of Mary's wretched life – Tidings of great joy indeed! When she never had sexual pleasure over him, he ran off to make trouble in the Temple, wandered away from home and neglected her, and finally she saw him killed.

What did he bring her but sorrow? Were the younger and naturally-born children any comfort?

31 December

I have only four events to record in 1962, that is to say only four I can remember:

Rob's death;

Matthei– perhaps of no importance;[90]

North Italy, with Tim;

Paris, St Rémy, Geneva, alone.

Locked Diary, 4 January
Robert Birley

Noel Annan's refusal to back a losing horse: he dismisses it as 'depressing'. Robert Birley,[91] who is leaving Eton for the Witwatersrand, is concerned by the South African government's attempted withdrawal of English from native Africans. He invites some of us to protest which I feel I should do, but N's liberalism does not carry him as far as that, though it takes him to lecture in Israel. When I praised Birley for leaving Eton for discomfort he pointed out that he did so only a year before the retiring age. I find some difficulty in discussing anything with him. He slips so rapidly from the fine into the sly. And he is fond of setting little traps towards which the obvious reaction will be the wrong one.

13 January
A list of the dead whom I miss or ought to

All Bodies Day falls this month if ever, and I ask myself 'Whom of the dead have I missed, or rather am I missing?' The list is short. Maimie, Mohammed el Adl, Francis Bennett, Aunt Rosie, Rose Macaulay, T.E. Lawrence and the lately lost Rob seem to complete it. If more occur, I will insert on the opposite page (Johnny Simpson, Bapu Sahib?). There are slight functional misses, like Agnes and Bone. There are those I should miss had they died sooner, like Masood and Frank Vicary, to whom H.O.M. is likely to be added. And there are those towards whom I feel piety and gratitude, headed by my mother.[92]

EMF to TWL, 25 January

I shall come to London to see you as soon as I can, but yes, it would be silly for me to travel in this weather and I have fixed myself to remain in or close to the college until the thaw comes. Since I returned here on 3 January I have got up only once. I miss you and other things badly, and dreary things like de Gaulle and Gaitskill's death take their places.

EMF to TWL, 30 January

Miss Perrin has retired, but her replacement, Mrs Richardson, though not an intellectual giant, is extremely nice, and enjoins cheerfulness by precept and example. When we talk together, as we often do, she always uses the last word of my sentence as the first word of hers, even if it is an intractable word like 'curious' or 'lamb'. So there is always formal continuity.

Wish there was more continuity between you and me. But we'll restore it.

January 1963 saw a notoriously savage winter. It would seem from our letters that between January and July there were many difficulties about meeting – almost all due to the weather. I recall that although the country had snow ploughs, many were iced into their garages.

Locked Diary, 10 February
Noel

Noel, admitting an Indian as fellow in the chapel the other evening, substituted 'In nomine Dei'[93] for the usual formula. The sort of imaginative sympathetic thing that no other provost would have thought of. What a complicated character! What a fascinating study of him could be written! What a job to sum him up!

Commonplace Book
His mother's ill-temper
The need to have someone to be kind to leads straight into a dubious aspect of Christianity and has to be watched. I think it was what damaged my mother after Gran's death[94] in that fated year 1911. I heard her moaning 'I could have made her so happy.' Her vengeful ill-temper auraed[95] each anniversary, setting in soon after the New Year and sometimes not clearing off till March. But I haven't made my point yet, which is that it is *right* to be kind and even sacrifice ourselves to people who need kindness and lie in our way.

15 April
A major worry
The death of our countryside [which will *never* be renewed] upsets me more than the death of a man or of a generation of men.

The next passage, from the *Locked Diary*, was first written in 1935, looked at again in 1958, and finally committed to the diary in 1963.

My Writings
Suppose I carry on with these notes in another form. I am fifty-six and have been told that Dr Norman Haire,[96] the sexologist, looks coy about my books, Hugh Walpole's,[97] Somerset Maugham's, and says that a scientific study of them would be fascinating but unpublishable. Well suppose

I try – not to be scientific but to say what I see. I want to love a strong young man of the lower classes and be loved by him and even hurt by him. That is my ticket, and then I have wanted to write respectable novels. No wonder they have worked out rather queer. The 'hurt by him' ought to be written in fainter ink. Although it is on my ticket, it is not as vivid as 'perfect union', and it is not underlined by the desire to be trodden on or shat on which characterises extreme cases. In the best love-making I have known there has been a sort of laughter and the most violent embrace gets softened by it. That's to say my problem as a writer hasn't been as awful as some's. It is these lower class youths, rather than any special antic with them, that has bothered me.

(N.B. I have never tried to turn a man into a girl, as Proust did with Albertine,[98] for this seemed derogatory to me as a writer.)

(Re-read without much interest when I am almost eighty.)

Adding when I am nearly eighty-five how <u>annoyed</u> I am with society for wasting my time by making homosexuality criminal. The subterfuges, the self consciousnesses that might have been avoided.

TWL to EMF, 22 July
I still feel uneasy that your last stay at P.F.[99] was not a happier one. The balance must be redressed, and I hope soon. I was, as you know and I've admitted, in something like a punch-drunk state about my work. It did overwhelm me for two months or so, and you found me in the middle of that period. In addition, at that precise moment I was also preoccupied with disentangling myself from a girl with

whom I'd become involved. This is the same girl with whom I'd come to Cambridge on Easter Monday and Tuesday, when I had not come to see you. I hadn't really wished you to meet her, merely because I wouldn't want to introduce to you any friend of mine whom I didn't have confidence in your liking. That time I didn't, and the nagging introspection which bothered me – at the time of your visit to Long Sutton – was why I had got involved with a girl whom I was disinclined to bring to see you (always assuming you were there). I've long since, ten days after your visit, closed that chapter and I've succeeded in rationalising the sequence of events, though not without some damage to my self-esteem.

Well, now events in my life have moved on with speed. I've just had a long letter from Ed Shils,[100] from Chicago, urging me towards an American university, and today a brief letter from Garry, who's been seeing Shils, in support of this. I have to make up my mind about this great decision, which if taken would surely determine my direction in life, in the next month or so.

Furthermore I have a new girl who has turned my mind towards marriage – though you alone now know this – more, and more seriously, than any other. She may not be as you would have expected. She is not at all like I would have, in advance guessing. She's not a graduate, but then she's suffered nine years of really bad health, with five serious operations and another, the worst, to come shortly. She's twenty-six, small, pretty, gay, and with admirable qualities of character that will, it seems, take her through anything. This is inadequate to describe her, and so I hope you will see her for yourself. She's half-convalescing at present, and mayn't be much in London.

EMF to TWL, 26 July

I am naturally delighted about the girl except when you speak (anyhow to yourself) of the possibility of marriage. I don't like that idea <u>at all</u> – you so poorly off and she in such poor health.

Locked Diary, 2 September
Bob & May

I am so saddened and changed by never seeing Bob – not since 23 July owing to careless planning, and not until 13 Sept. Same applying to May. I can't expect to meet them just as usual. And William[101] will come with me, and his winsomeness will intervene and distort.

EMF to TWL, 3 September

I'm afraid I can't alter my opinion until the situation alters. It is an Euclidian opinion – nothing moral or emotional in it.

Question: if two people are not rich and one of them unwell, is marriage wise? Answer: no.

Question: if health is restored should they marry? Answer: yes.

Locked Diary, 5 September
Tiredness; Tim

Surely above date must be earlier. Doesn't matter but I want to record that on the night of 3–4 September I was <u>dead</u> tired in my flat, and the words must be taken literally. It wasn't comfortable, like being <u>nearly</u> dead at Addenbrooke's during my illness. When I did sleep it was until eleven the next morning and Tim had been ringing me up.

He seems determined to marry a 'gallant' little invalid who may destroy him.[102]

9 September
Noel

Provost Noel Annan <u>is</u> awful and shall be scarified by a firmer pen. Hearing that Desmond Shaw Taylor[103] etc. had been kind to me and treated me with distinction he began – characteristically – considering giving a little dinner to us as a group. Proust could have done him, and in past days I could have recreated a character from my impressions of him, as I did Mrs Failing[104] from Uncle Willie. He's certainly the person who has most interested me clinically during the last two years; if during that period I had ever been entertained at the lodge[105] my interest might be slighter.

I have elsewhere indicated the elevated quality of his snobbery; he pursues people not because they have done things but because they might do them.

20 September
Noel

Reopening, I find to my amusement that I want again to discuss our provost. He really <u>is</u> a shit. I visited Angus Wilson[106] yesterday who certainly conciliated me with distinguished treatment, also said he would like to give some warnings to Noel about the B.M.[107] to which he has been appointed. The message has been ill received. Subject having been changed, 'Was he laying down the law as usual?' Politics is mentioned. 'I didn't know he took part in them. I know of course that he was an ordinary liberal of the middle of the road.' Writings despised.[108]

September 1963: Great concern over my engagement.

25 September
The countryside; Bob; Tim
I am in low spirits, partly old age which is natural, partly because the countryside, in this and other countries is doomed. Neither the commercialisation of art nor the destruction of individualism upsets me so much.

Evening Entry: How can I control my moods? This morning I was wretched thinking of Bob's ill health and illish temper and approaching x-ray. Now I am quite resilient – enjoyed seeing the Richards,[109] also warm call from Garry Runciman and we talked guardedly but in agreement over Tim's engagement. And I have done a little work on the radio script for *Howards End*. Deaf in hall as generally, no matter.

5 November
Ben; Brian Remnant; music
Thirty-five years older than Ben, I have just received his birthday tribute. I wish I could have contributed something more personal, as Rostropovitch[110] has. Oh what Ben has held up for us, and without smugness. I don't care if I never see him again. 'I must see you again' belongs to the lower air.

I pass away and everything else will, but I have faith in friends and unspiritual happiness. Brian Remnant, Eric and Nancy Crozier,[111] Eric F. of course, Kenneth passes, H.O.M. ditto, Mattei, Reg[112] – an actually grateful letter. And the obvious and often honoured. It's a lateral feeling – we all go neither up nor down, but drift, and recognise and love each other for a time.

How I miss my life in music, which ceased when Aldeburgh did. It had a warmth and vitality which Life in

Literature has lacked. For anyone who survives from it my heart beats: e.g. for the Croziers three days ago.

On 22 November President Kennedy was assassinated, a tragedy that, I believe, affected most people of my generation. I was at a folk concert at Cecil Sharp House and at the interval we heard that Kennedy had been shot. At the end we heard that he was dead. It was a catastrophic blow to what had seemed to be a fresh, vigorous, liberal and intelligent approach to the world.

EMF to TWL, 29 November

My high spot has been Ben's *Gloriana*[113] and his birthday party at the Harewoods'[114] afterwards. Since the date was the 22nd you will wonder how this can be, but we were miraculously preserved from knowledge of what had happened earlier in the day. I can't imagine that anyone who knew could have managed to conceal it. It was a sort of respite. Now came the squalor and the chatter that follow after wickedness with the police etc. scuttling for position.

Christmas I may stay here, very quietly, which I like. My mother also liked a quiet Christmas, but never got it through too much compassion and fidgeting.

The old Pitt Press is to be pulled down to make a car tower – thus destroying the loveliest prospect in Cambridge – the view from the steps on the south side of the Senate House. It can't be called a public view, so there can't be good ground for an appeal.

Locked Diary, 30 November
Tim et al.

Panged at realising how many friends are slipping away – Tim, Kenneth, Nick, Lindsay, Carlos possibly. Paul

Cadmus.[115] I have written to Tim and will to the others. There seems no reason in any case beyond the weakening of facilities. Ben is safe, since his birthday, though I am unlikely to see him.

31 December
The year's end
It begins to look as if the New Year will be seen in at Coventry by me, Bob, May, tolerably Silvia, and less tolerably by two friendly cits[116] called Jack and Pam. I had rather we had been alone.

Long loving ridiculous letter from Joe which May was reading aloud to our laughter when the visitors rang.

EMF to TWL, January
I certainly should like to be with you alone for a bit – not that I have anything special to say, but we have so often been alone happily together in the past.

Here comes Mr Iredale[117] to play the piano – or is it the violin? – with a young man who plays the violin – or is it the piano? at a forthcoming local concert. I shall take the opportunity to 'rest' in the other room.

My great excitement is *Billy Budd*. I got both to the dress rehearsal and the first night – marvellous. Ben greatly pleased. They have arrived and are at it. Quite competent. It is for an old folks' home.

Locked Diary, 29 February
The New Year
Billy Budd – vowed to open with those words but write them two months late. And *Towards Probation*, Bob's autobiography which our friendship has helped him to write.

Not many can start a year, and their eighty-sixth one, with such good reasons for pleasure. And for distress with the complete break up of Eric's home.[118]

EMF to TWL, 11 March
I love you and may all happiness be yours. It may be worth stating at such a moment that I have loved my life. [Morgan was eighty-five]

On 21 March I got married, to a woman of whom Morgan disapproved, although he had never spoken to me directly about this, only about her health issues. I regret that he did not.

I believed that the psychological problems associated with her health problems would be dispersed by the security of marriage. However, he was proved right, in that I was divorced some years later.[119]

As a wedding present he gave me 'something personal if the right trifle occurs'. It was life membership of the London Library, a present that I could enjoy for the rest of my life.

Locked Diary, 25 March
Ivan Ilyitch

Last Sunday read *Ivan Ilyitch*[120] in the train. The horror of ending or of being extinguished fortunately has not yet come upon me. And when pain comes – as it probably will – nothing I record will have value.

16 May
Various people

I have been thinking with sadness that unless one starts off with intimacy – as I have done more or less with Narliker[121] and with Drum and did with irretrievable Kenneth[122] – it is impossible to know a colleague well. The years I have lived at King's, the little I have reaped or presumably sown! Things still go on outside it. I have of course never worked in the community or given it anything beyond Aunt Laura's[123] date. And the starts I have made inside it – Lindsay Heather, Tim Leggatt, Bryan Remnant – have not flourished when transplanted outside. It has been of the greatest practical use, for which I am grateful.

I take it that Morgan regretted that his relations with the three of us did not develop in an intimate direction. He once said to me, after I'd stayed a night in his Chiswick flat, 'If things had been different, we could have slept together', to which I could only reply, 'Yes', recognising that there was an enduring homosexual attraction from his side. I like to think that, after this, Jonathan is right, Morgan regarded me not as a possible homosexual partner, but as more akin to Fielding.[124]

EMF to TWL, 25 May
Off to St Rémy
But my travelling with you, both in England, Wales slightly, and Italy come to mind, and I want to thank you for making them so pleasant.

EMF to TWL, 5 June
I had such a nice meal with you both. Also a nice one next day with Garry and Ruth. I get on so easily with him in these days. I wish we had met more in the past.

Locked Diary, 26 June
The Longest Journey
Sixty years ago next September I paid my first visit to Figsbury Rings[125] which were the heart of the *The Longest Journey*. The day before yesterday I paid the last. William Golding drove me as near to them as he could and I could have had a worse companion. It was a grey day which I do not mind in Wiltshire and we saw two blue butterflies which are everywhere else extinct. The second displayed itself, open winged and heroically large at the entrance to the inner circle. The rings are heroically larger than I thought – I remember them smaller and trimmer and perhaps turnipped. Their grass was tousled and sopping wet and through their wide entrance-gaps Wiltshire drifted into the invisible, which was not far off and included the spire of Salisbury. A

<u>huge</u> place, then. My other lapse of memory was the tree in the centre, which is two trees and not central. The lame shepherd boy – did I fantastically transfer his lameness to Rickie? It was a marvellous scramble and my lameness – another quaintness? – eased off and didn't return till the next day.

I am not sure whether Golding, if he had known any of the above, would have been arrested by it. He has a strong and strange and not uncongenial imagination, but so pivoted on the sense of sin that it might only [have] caught (and condemned) the homosexual whiff. I exclaimed several times that the area was marvellous, only large – larger than I recalled. I was filled with thankfulness and security and glad that I had given myself so much back. The butterfly was a moving glint, and I shall lie in Stephen's arms instead of his child. How I wish that book hadn't faults! But they do not destroy it, and the gleam, the greatness, the grass remain. I don't want any other coffin.

11 July
Mattei

No doubt it is Mattei's disaster[126] that stops me from concentrating. It happened on the 6th, he told me about it in the Reform on the 9th, case heard on the 21st. I am so distressed at his ill luck and a little at my own. I shall soon hear whether I have to offer to speak for his character in court. I do not much mind for my own at eighty-five.

12 July
Various

Mattei's disaster, Bob's foot, Eric's silence and unhappiness, Ted's dangerous desultoriness, Joe and Jack's endangered holiday[127] through the air strike: do add up (and add Tim's virtual banishment) and pull me down even though I am all right in myself.

23 July
A daily routine
In this curious period I follow a rhythm so definite that it can be foreseen. I wake up feeling absolutely awful and sometimes with the jump that has attended past upsets. The ill-fates of my friends – Bob, Mattei, Joe, Eric – are topmost – and under them my own unpleasant fate on 1 July 1965 when the college rebuilding[128] will start and break up all amenity. I get more neutral after morning-tea is served by my good bed-maker, despair weakens while I bathe and dress, and if my post is not too bad – and thanks to the strike there is not much of it – I gradually pull myself together and am alert and polite to other humans. So far so good, but there is much better to come. In the afternoon I am crowned with curiosity and a capacity for pleasure – aesthetic and intellectual pleasure. I want to approach Shakespeare, Wordsworth and at this moment Blake, Verdi etc – to get closer to them, to learn more of them and to redate them. And, joined with this cheerful inhumanity is my old faith in the individual whom I still love, still try to help – at present by money gifts because I have heaps of money.

EMF to TWL, 26 July
Dear dear Tim… What I should particularly like, if you can spare it, is an evening alone with you. Not that either of us would have anything particular to say, but it would be a sort of continuation of our times together in the past, and very welcome to me. <u>If</u> you can fix it… Look in your diary, clear

your head (mine is not wholly translucent) and see what can be done.

Commonplace Book, post-July
Greek and Latin
Main reason for retaining them in education: they remind youths and maidens that there is a civilisation and a way of looking at things which was not and could not be Christian. Since at eighty-five I may have to die soon, I should like to emphasise that I am still not Christian and don't want even a memorial service in our friendly chapel.

Locked Diary, 3 August
H.O.M.
Have just heard that H.O.M. died suddenly, on 31 July, in his home.[129] Have looked at the Virgil he gave me when I was twenty-one.

The marvellous fortnight must be dated for mnemonic reasons, though all that glorified it, all that I saw felt heard thought has already escaped.

{Aug 14 – 17 – K Clark, Saltwood
{Aug 18 – 20 – N. Scarf,[130] Shinglestreet
{Aug 20 – 22 – Ben's, Aldeburgh
{Aug 22 – 24 – Bill's, Aldburgh
{Aug 25 – 28 – Eric, here

September
Lindsay Heather
My own day has been coloured by a visit from Lindsay Heather, who left me liking him again. He is making a failure of his career – still worrying what his voice is and changing teachers, still failing to create but knowing what

creation is. Off for a year to Munich with a grant from the German Government. To do what?[131] He was affectionate, handsome and selfish – towards the end I discovered that he has had and perhaps still has infected bladder and kidney, and it is this that tipped me back into liking him. June (his wife) goes with him to Munich, but he showed no desire to mention her. I think his heart was broken in Italy. His stammer was as bad as ever when he arrived, but went away as soon as he found me friendly. He was carelessly and splendidly dressed on the quiet side of loudness. Very civil and considerate. Kissed.

TWL to EMF, 15 September

I am sorry that we disappeared so suddenly last Tuesday, making our leave-taking so abrupt: although I always feel this is better than a protracted good-bye. Thank you so much for the highly civilised and delightful lunch, and thank you quite especially for our very good evening together the previous day. It was wonderful to have a long talk and to range over the various trips and holidays that we have shared, remembering the small instances with which our memories of those occasions are stored. It was almost like being in Italy again, finding the hotel in Cremona, being waited on in the Vicenza restaurant by Sir Adrian Boult,[132] re-living the agony of our exchanges with the Seguso Medusa.

I am sorry that I am going away at this time. It is very sad not being able to plan a next meeting within a month or so, and not to be here when, for example, Chetwynd Court[133] (I hope I remember the name right) is pulled apart beneath your window. However, we shall write as we did before and I hope that will speed the time of being away.

The greatest part always remains unsaid. Fortunately we both know this and don't have to fumble at trying to say it. To be close to you is still as great a joy as it has ever been.

In September my wife and I went to Chicago, for me to work towards a Ph.D. in the Sociology Division of the University of Chicago. When I left India, I had the idea of becoming an anthropologist, but I found that I couldn't do so without having a first degree in anthropology, which I thought would take too long. But while at PEP, I discovered that American universities did not require the first degree, and I shifted from Anthropology to Sociology, in the belief that this would be more useful for a life in politics, my new ambition.

Locked Diary, 12 October
Patrick & Sydney
I have felt in good form no odd or giddy feelings, have finished Book I of *Anna Karenina*... It was nice to see Patrick and Sydney receiving in the absent Provost's drawing room, and to feel Sydney kissing Dr Forster's cheek.

TWL to EMF, 11 October
From the University of Chicago.
We had a smooth, uneventful voyage out, which did have the merit of separating departure and arrival in New York. We spent two days in New York, where we visited the Guggenheim Museum and the Natural History Museum. The Guggenheim you must have seen pictures of, Frank Lloyd Wright's snail-shaped building in which you walk down a wide spiral staircase looking at the pictures as you go. I didn't like the building itself – it's rather meringue-like in outside appearance – nor its style of display. The current

exhibition, of modern American drawings, had some interesting design-like drawings and some atrocious stuff – I thought. We went to the Natural History Museum on Jonathan Miller's suggestion (we had a most lively lunch with him) and found it a delight. It consists in a series of tableaux behind glass of animals, birds, flowers and trees – as detailed as natural scenes and lifelike to an uncanny degree. They are powerful stimulants to the imagination, and remind one of what non-industrialised nature is like.

And so to Chicago. The University is about six miles south of the city centre, of which we've seen little. The University area is most attractive. It is made up of streets almost all lined with an abundance of trees, which are just turning from green. The private houses are many of them very prettily painted, mostly of wood: the blocks of flats are not obtrusive. It is a wholly middle-class district, but largely negro, so that the precincts of the campus are racially quite mixed – and happily so. The University buildings are grey gothic, redolent of the English tradition.

The great bulk of the students are graduate students, which gives a research emphasis to the departments and a generally earnest tone. I am well impressed with Janowitz,[134] the professor under whose auspices (apart from Shils') I am here and who also seems to be the most stimulating person. I've not yet an assessment of my fellow-students, but there are evidently few only who are exceptional for intellect. As I've written, I have to attend lectures, indeed eight a week are compulsory effectively. This is no bad thing for me, who am in need of making up for not having a first degree in Sociology.

Thank you very much for your letter and the news of your good health: the letter followed us here of course.

We do not have much news of England. Even the *New York Times* only has what amounts to headline news. So the election is very remote from us, crucial as it so clearly is. The election campaign here is going steadily on, but opinion seems generally to be agreed that President Johnson will be re-elected. However, I must write my first impressions of America in another letter.

Locked Diary, 19 November
Ill in Addenbrooke's

I liked the private ward as a whole but was oversensitive to anything bossy or nursified. I am sure to have to go in again and must try to keep myself in hand. What moves me is the goodness of my friends. Bob and May came naturally, Joe too, Patrick and Sydney much – a boy called ??? from up this staircase A.

EMF to TWL, 29 November

Here all is comfort and calm. I go to Ben's at Aldeburgh for Christmas, thence to Bob and May's at Coventry for the New Year plus a few days at Rockingham Castle. All very pleasant. I haven't been immediately well. Six days in Addenbrooke's, no point in mentioning it to most people but I wish to do so to you. Slight brain-muddle. It didn't extend beyond failing to remember addresses and even that is clearing up. Everyone has been so kind to me here and I continue to enjoy life uninterruptedly. Such a marvellous concert in the chapel two nights back – Beethoven's *Missa Solemnis*.[135] I have heard it before but never been so stunned. The violin solo, or rather intrusion, towards the end is I suppose the most original. One scarcely notices its entrance but after a time listens backwards and feels there is nothing like it in music. But the close of the *Gloria* stuns too.

I am also involved (aesthetically) with K.Clark's[136] book on Ruskin, which he has just sent me. It is partly an anthology, for which he has been gathering for some time. But this is attended by a remarkable essay which should rehabilitate R. He faces the fact that R was constantly silly, puts it aside which no one else has done, and examines what is left. Which is most impressive and heartening. I think it's a book that will make a change.

Locked Diary, 31 December
Reflections on 1964
Shall be eighty-six in four or five hours, and am where I would best be for the event, namely Bob and May's Coventry house.

I jotted down the chief events of the year on a little piece of paper which I have lost. – Have here found it. – The French holiday in May was good. Movements were dull and limited otherwise and my recent superindisposition obscures them. I have no pains, sure friends, and a fairish past. I should have been a more famous writer if I had written or rather published more, but sex has prevented the latter.[137]

Locked Diary, 4 January
The change of year
Rockingham Castle, eighty-six years and four days old, and well except for a pit-a-pat heart this morning, promoted by fussing up and down the stairs. I feel it indeed as I write and must be careful.

19 March
Bob
Much inclines me to aloofness, the loss of memory, e.g., and I have had to make a list of drawbacks. I have not liked the aloofness of Bob. Our severance has been harmful. Not a happy visit to Coventry on the whole. He was sometimes kind and very so, but only when he had decided to be so. He allows others to initiate nothing.

TWL to EMF, 8 May
I have just heard from my father of your illness. I am distraught to be so far away from you. I am so sorry this has happened. I do hope you are comfortable and well looked-after. I am sure that Bob and May are taking good care that you are. I send you all my wishes for your comfort and recovery.

I think often of the happiness I have had on our trips together, never more so than in the summer. The winter anywhere is a time of intermission and reflections – and nowhere more so than in Chicago: the summer is the time of expansion, when one is wide open to experience and joy. Summer came here last week, and with it, for me, the surge of summer memories. It is quite simply true that our trips to Italy and Herefordshire are clearest and most important to me. They are well-defined and marked by many specific memories of shared experience. I don't only think of the treats like Kilpeck church or *Tosca* in Verona, but of many seemingly trivial things like the horrible old woman who shouted at us in the Pensione Seguso or our experience with the gondolier. I feel sure you remember things in much this way too. As time goes by, a great mosaic of remembrances is built up which is the most essential part of one's self, that part shared with people whom one loves.

You will know that, although I am a great way off in space, I always feel close to you in understanding and love. I hope this quick letter will overcome some of the distance. I will write again soon. Meanwhile I hope you will recover all your strength.

I send my love in very special measure.

Locked Diary, 6 June
Ill

Have been reading in *Howards End* and the *Passage*. Both very good. There is no doubt that I have been very good and deserve my present position and its attendance [sic] nonsenses. Stroke at Coventry on 3 April. Great kindnesses here, even from servants I don't know by sight or name, have led me to honour smallness. If two people were agreeable to each other 500 years ago it does matter, whatever historians or sociologists say. I <u>don't</u> die in despair, at least so far not, and I am thankful not to be preparing for death. I wish the world had got better but with the growth of the population and the supremacy of money it can't.

EMF to TWL, July
After an illness

It is about time I answered your touching and helpful letter of May, written when you heard of my illness. And a previous of March may be by no means ignored.

I have made a good recovery. I skilfully lay in Bob and May's sympathetic sitting room until the end of the month, since when I have been here [Cambridge]. I enjoy life very much, while respectfully admitting that others may have a more commanding grasp of it. Music remains supreme. All July there is a promising 'Festival' in Cambridge and I am going to about seven things – the summits from my point of view being Monteverdi's *Orfeo* and Verdi's *Requiem* – the latter in Ely cathedral to which David Willcocks[138] most sweetly drives me over. I can't read a lot or walk a lot, but you must allow that I have done pretty well. I often think of me and you in Italy.

I am writing, believe it or not, in your former bedroom, looking towards the sunlit chapel, which is not often so lit. Jayant Narlikar, who now occupies the set, allows me to thus use it, so that I may escape the noise and devastation behind. For Hell has broken loose and is to continue for at least two years – the college building scheme I mean. The college has been awfully good to me – double glazed all my windows – bedroom – sitting room and bathroom – but they all look into Chetwynd Court, which is now full of sheds. The lovely almond trees have gone, and worse still the immemorial mulberry in Webbs.[139] Noise and dust are inevitable. So I can't be too grateful to my considerate and delightful Indian neighbour. He is an astronomer who works with Hoyle and though only in his twenties is already famous.

Much love and do not forget me. I do not expect you will and I shall never forget you. – Sorry my handwriting is so wobbly, but I am lucky to have got back what I have. *Howards End* has been dramatised and will terminate the 'Cambridge Festival' – I have been very anxious about it, but they are taking immense trouble and I think it won't go badly.

Locked Diary, 16 July
Ill

I am ill or anyhow on the odd side of health and must go to my bed – having incidentally asked the date of good Narlikar next door. All is well, or seems to be better than it is with most men of eighty-six – Bob and May try to come to the play (H.E.)[140] next week, I have not yet seen it myself, expect to but don't much want to. They can't get a good Leonard Bast is the latest, also the circular stage is too large.

At this point my wife and I took a trip from Chicago out to California. It was an immense journey, taking in Yellowstone National Park, Salt Lake City, Las Vegas, Yosemite National Park, the so-often filmed vistas of Arizona, the Grand Canyon and old Indian sites in Colorado.

EMF to TWL, 4 November

I see nothing startling here in the way of scenery, but a good deal that is startling in the way of architecture. The new section of the college is being built outside my windows between me and Queen's, a huge gap has developed. You would think that the noise must be awful, but no, the college has given me four double windows and they practically exclude all annoyance. Indeed, after building on building falls the expanse becomes more and more dramatic. Building after building will presently arise, but the results then will be what we shall see.

Locked Diary, 15 December
Garry

Interesting and welcome call from Garry Runciman, whom I like, and nearly told him so and kissed him, which would have been inept. My defences are slackening, no doubt as the result of illness. Why should I inflict details of my illness on a stranger? G is being drawn into the paternal business – unless he is careful.

My walking and talking better. Reading poor.

EMF to TWL, 5 February
My wife

My relations with her have always been so pleasant, but my deepest strongest and largest feelings are for you, and I wish to make that clear.

I go on all right, and can now walk without a stick. My real bother is my eyesight, which is unlikely to improve. Have just had a word with Ed Shils. How good he has been helping you!

Locked Diary, 10 March
Edmund Leach and Patrick

This afternoon the college elected Edmund Leach[141] as provost – to be informed immediately afterwards that he had had a dangerous operation and was still ill at Papworth.[142] What a mess-up, especially for the young who had insisted on him and had rejected Patrick as too old. In a couple of hours I go to *Measure for Measure* with dear Anne McBurney. Only a loathsome man could have written it, and I begin to think Shakespeare must have written it.[143]

At this point, applying from Chicago, I obtained an appointment as a lecturer in Sociology at the University of Sussex.

EMF to TWL, 9 April
Provost Leach; Noel

Brighton is certainly a pleasant prospect. I hear of it, and of Keele, as the two best of the new universities. And the site is said to be charming.

Leach seems to be an excellent appointment. I have known him slightly through the Humanists. He was the young people's choice and they had a great majority. The older people suggested Patrick, who characteristically supported Leach, and I think all are now pleased.

Noel, to write more privately, hasn't been a great success in my opinion. He was only interested in the clever, and Gaby in the end wasn't even interested in them, and stayed mainly in London. Noel should do excellently in London and has spoken splendidly in the Lords about homosexuality.

There were several other letters here, but none worth quoting.

Locked Diary, 16 July
At Bob's and very happy to be so. Not very robust. Can scarcely see to write but music okay.

25 July
At Rockingham
Sudden suspicion that I am 'at the end of my tether'. Slight head-feeling yesterday the only evidence of it and but for the endless cold should be cheerful. Faith is slaving at her novel. I have retired to my bedroom.

29 July
The College
Delighted, when entering my room this morning, to run into Mrs Richardson,[144] who uttered a cry of delight. It is always nice to be liked, and I know that I often am, but it is seldom that one receives a spontaneous cry, and seldom at all from a bed-maker. It is a precious gift, which few receive

or are interested in receiving, and one gets it by just going on as one wants. Joined to my success in literature it makes me feel that my life was creditable though in my dotage I can scarcely write or read, and though some of my friends (I instance Ben who called today) no longer honour me. They remain so creative – Mrs Richardson ranks me with her mother almost. I shall never forget that cry of delight.

14 September
Ivan Ilyitch
On Saturday Bob fetches me back to Coventry, or so I hope, but I am prone to hope. An American visitor has been trying to read *Ivan Ilyitch* aloud to me. What a good story it is especially the opening chapter, after his death. In some ways I don't want to be alive, in other ways and to be with friends I do.

I managed to complete my Ph.D. work, courses and research, in just two years, when most students took five. I was driven extremely hard by Professor Janowitz. As we said goodbye, he said to me, 'Now you will have to start working' – after I had worked myself to the limit to complete the Ph.D. in an extraordinarily short time. He meant of course that I would now have to study to be ahead of my students, as I taught courses that I had never taken. He was right. I had a lectureship in Sociology at the University of Sussex, and in September I returned to England, to a flat in Brighton.

Morgan and I had problems meeting from autumn 1966 onward. He lived between King's and Coventry. We exchanged quite a few letters, but some were rather muddled. Many were written for him by the Buckinghams as his handwriting became worse and worse.

EMF to TWL, 9 November

<u>What</u> news, and what ever have you been up to?[145] Over-work of course, and will it give you a lesson? I hope so, though not confidently. I imagine that you should be out soon, and that a good rest will set you up, but do not over-work again. The human frame, constructed by God, will not stand it. I had so looked forward to seeing you here on Saturday. But that is only a local disappointment. The important thing is to get well and to do this quickly. I will go now and get some tea, and shall drink it thinking of you.

EMF to TWL, 1 December

I stay here over the New Year, and in great comfort, by which time the worst of the rebuilding in King's should be over. I have a nice new staircase coming up into what was the guest room and they are propping up my floor. The college and the people in it are very agreeable but architecturally the scene is not very inviting.

Locked Diary, 27 March
Ill health

Have been here since January, and before that at Addenbrooke's for almost a fortnight. Things might be much worse. It was another stroke I think. ('Here' by the way is at Bob's.) I should be here till early June, when we should go to Aldeburgh Arts Festival. After that nothing or perhaps nothing indeed. But I am very pleased to have lived so long and without degradation.

May Buckingham to TWL, 9 May

We manage to get quite a lot of visitors for him. Earlier this week we had Quentin Bell[146] who will be joining you in the autumn and will look you up.

Morgan has no plans apart from Aldeburgh and after that he will be either in King's or here with us and of course he hopes to be mostly in King's with his possessions around him.

Locked Diary, 6 June
Joe

Joe died suddenly and we think painless in his flat last Saturday.[147] He is cremated on Friday I think and has slipped out of life as easily as he could wish. Has had no interest since Queenie (that awful dog) died. I feel so strangely about him. He cared for no one yet was so good to them and extremely intelligent.

I am probably close to the end of my own life, which has been a successful one and to the end a happy one. And now for dinner!

1968

Commonplace Book, 11 November
No more to write
Doubtful whether I shall write more. Have ordered this book to go to College Library.

I had quite a number of letters from Morgan during the year. They were almost entirely about plans to meet, but it seems that we never did. The letters were mostly written by May Buckingham, with very scratchy lines from Morgan. Here is an example.

EMF to TWL, 22 December
I look forward to seeing you on the 4th and I hope that by then all will still be well.

I will not write more now as I am now on the stupid side but quite bright in my particular way.

1969

Morgan turned ninety on 1 January, when he was awarded an O.M. in the New Year honours list. The College gave an excellent lunch in honour of his ninetieth birthday. It was quite a small and private affair, to which I was delighted to go. He was in good form and I believe he enjoyed himself.

Bob Buckingham to TWL, 7 July

He is very well considering his age, much more feeble than a few months ago and his sight is getting worse but he still enjoys music and listens to gramophone records with enjoyment. We all send our love and look forward to seeing you and Emily in the not too distant future.

EMF to TWL, 12 August

I'm having an easy life, but not a very active one, and it is one of my friends who is writing my letter for me. I'm stopping with him and his people until the end of the month.

Best love to you both and to you all, for naturally I include your baby. You tell me little about her, but I get the impression that she is charming.

Morgan again with his best love.

His last written words to me. I had planned to take my daughter Emily, born on 19 March 1969, to show him on 19 September. I don't remember if I did.

Bob Buckingham to TWL, 7 June
I am sorry to tell you that Morgan died here at 2.40 a.m. today. He was taken ill at King's on 22 May and came to us on the 27th. He had a slight stroke but gradually deteriorated. His end was quite peaceful and May nursed him to the end. He is to be cremated here according to his wishes with no ceremony.

Bob Buckingham to TWL, 13 June
Morgan was cremated here yesterday with just a few personal friends present and the vice-provost of King's.[148] His death was very quiet and peaceful, no pain, just a slow gentle growing weakness. I was so thankful we were able to care for him to the end. Just as he had wished.

A few months before his death in 1967, Joe Ackerley wrote an obituary of Morgan which he left with the *Observer* for future use. Its climactic sentence ran:

I would say that in so far as it is possible for any human being to be both wise and worldly wise, to be selfless in any material sense, to have no envy, jealousy, vanity, conceit, to contain no malice, no hatred (though he had anger), to be always reliable, considerate, generous, never cheap, Morgan came as close to that as can be got.

On 6 July 1981, a plaque was placed on 11 Salisbury Avenue, Coventry, and unveiled by May Buckingham. It read as follows:

E.M. FORSTER
1879–1970

Lived often in later years at 11, Salisbury Avenue, Coventry,
the home of his friends Robert and May Buckingham, and
died here on 7th June 1970.

There was a brief ceremony, which I was very pleased to
attend.

I take this opportunity to consider why Forster wrote no more novels after *A Passage to India*. Of course he did write short stories, of which two have been mentioned in this memoir, 'The Torque' and 'The Other Boat'; and the eighty-two pages of the 1951 revision of *Arctic Summer*. He writes that sex prevented him from *publishing* more, not from writing more. Why then did he write no more novels, after 1924, when he was only forty-five?

In his magisterial biography, Nick Furbank suggests three reasons.[149] First, that Forster was superstitious, and that after great success – with *A Passage to India* and *Aspects of the Novel* – he feared that he would be unable to maintain this quality in his writing. Indeed the reason that Furbank named the second volume of Morgan's biography *Polycrates' Ring* was that Morgan had drawn T.E. Lawrence's attention to the story in which Polycrates, invariably successful in all that he did, was advised by his friend, the king of Egypt, who was disturbed by so much good fortune, to sacrifice something of great value to himself. Polycrates threw a precious ring into the sea, but days later it reappeared in the belly of a fish.[150]

Second, that he was bored of writing about marriage and heterosexual relations. However, this did not prevent him, after writing *Maurice* (1910–14), from starting *Arctic Summer* (1911–2), which he later revised in 1951, and above all from starting *A Passage to India* in 1915 and completing it, after the war, in 1922.

Third, that 'he received his whole inspiration – a vision, a kind of plot, a message – all at once, in early manhood' and that 'his inspiration as a novelist always harked back to that moment of enlightenment'.[151] But what was this inspiration, this vision, this moment of enlightenment? We do not know.

Forster's latest biographer, Wendy Moffat,[152] strongly suggests that it was no longer necessary for him to write novels once he had established a number of fully-fledged homosexual relationships and of no interest to write about heterosexual relationships.

I don't myself set great store by all these suppositions, although there may well be truth in Furbank's first and third suggestions. They do not seem to have been born out by Morgan himself. I take very seriously his statement in 1959: 'I wanted to write but did not want to write novels'.

Forster's most sensitive and intelligent critic is Frank Kermode, in various articles, but especially in *Concerning E.M. Forster*.[153] In this he writes: 'While *A Passage to India* was still new, he told Siegfried Sassoon he would never write another novel – "my patience with ordinary people has given out" – though he declared his intention to go on writing.' And indeed he did go on writing: reviews, broadcasts, diaries and, of course, letters.[154] But why did he make the decision in 1924? I believe it was because he considered *A Passage to India* to be his supreme achievement, and one that he could not surpass.

Forster did think that there was much muddle in life – and frequently said so.[155] What he meant was that we are not in control of our lives; there is much ambiguity, and we frequently and inevitably misinterpret what is happening. And he felt that this was very evidently true in India. His experience with the Maharajah of Dewas was surely especially convincing, hence the incident in the Marabar caves in *A Passage to India*. When Morgan was asked what happened in the caves and said 'I don't know', he was being truthful rather than impatient.[156] In real life one often doesn't know what has happened; one just goes along with what one thinks is the likeliest interpretation.

The third part of *A Passage to India* – 'Temple' – enabled him to show an Indian muddle. Sometimes I think this is a little overdone. For example:

> Rose-leaves fall from the houses, sacred spices and coco-nut are brought forth... It was the half-way moment; the God had extended his Temple, and paused exultantly. Mixed and confused in their passage, the rumours of salvation entered the Guest House. They were startled and moved on to the porch, drawn by the sudden illumination. The bronze gun up on the fort kept flashing, the town was a blur of light, in which the houses seemed dancing and the palace waving little wings. The water below, the hills and sky above, were not involved as yet; there was still only a little light and song struggling among the shapeless lumps of the universe. The song became audible through much repetition; the choir was repeating and inverting the names of deities.[157]

This is superb writing, but 'mixed and confused in their passage', 'waving little wings' and 'the lumps of the universe' don't mean very much, and I think one is left with the impression that much of what is taken seriously in India is in fact hilarious. This, I believe, is where my friend Bishnu Dey parted company with Morgan[158] and where I do, just as I part company with David Lean whose Alec Guinness as Godbole didn't seem to me to work at all.[159]

There are two aspects of Morgan that identify him as a man and as an author. First, he was a creative artist and he strove all his life to be so. This means that his aim was to combine realism with the spiritual, the mythical, the magical, for only by doing so could any orderliness[160] be brought into this muddled world. Morgan wrote of the artist, 'the one thing which he, and he alone, can do – the making of something out of words or sounds or paint or clay or marble or steel or film which has internal harmony and presents order to a permanently disarranged planet.' And again, 'Works of art, in my opinion, are the only objects in the material universe to possess internal order.'[161]

Second, Morgan believed in personal relations, on the one hand, as Kermode puts it, as the cure for unbelief, and on the other, as the supreme opportunity to express love. In his most famous essay, 'What I Believe' (1939), he writes strongly in favour of democracy which focuses on the individual, promotes creativity in all areas, accepts criticism and makes civilisation most possible. 'So Two cheers for Democracy: one because it admits variety and two because it permits criticism. Two cheers are quite enough: there is no occasion to give three. Only Love the Beloved Republic deserves that.'[162]

He did not distinguish between homosexual and heterosexual love, and he never intimated any such distinction to me. Indeed he took a considerable interest in my heterosexual relationships.

A Passage to India ends superbly.

'Why can't we be friends now?' said [Fielding to Aziz], holding him affectionately. 'It's what I want. It's what you want.' But the horses didn't want it – they swerved apart; the earth didn't want it, sending up rocks through which riders must pass single file; the temples, the tank, the jail, the palace, the birds, the carrion, the Guest House [...] they didn't want it, they said in their hundred voices, 'No, not yet,' and the sky said, 'No, not there.'[163]

We do not control our lives and they are something of a muddle.

What other novel was there for him to write?

NOTES

1. Sir John Tressider Sheppard was a Cambridge University lecturer in Classics, fellow of King's from 1908 and provost of King's 1933–54. He was provost when I took the entrance exam in 1951.

2. King's College Chapel. Its building began in the fifteenth century but was not finished until well into the sixteenth.

3. Agnes Dowland, engaged by Morgan's mother as a parlour maid in 1904, she stayed forty years; Ivor Ramsay (1902–56); clerical dean of King's; threw himself from the chapel roof on 22 January 1956, during my time as an undergraduate; Stephen Glanville (1900–56) was Cambridge professor of Egyptology and then provost of King's 1954–6, during my first two years in the college; Sydney Wilkinson (1923–2005) was the wife of L.P. (Patrick) Wilkinson (1907–95), Classics scholar and senior tutor of King's 1946–56, including my first two years in the college; Kenneth Harrison, university lecturer in Biochemistry, was a very close friend of Morgan's. His father was chancellor of York Minster; Johnny Hampson Simpson (1901–55) in 1925 became nurse to a mentally disabled boy. Forster came to know him in 1932 and considered him a saint-like character.

4. Robert J. (Bob) Buckingham (1904–75), from a very poor background, joined the police in the mid-1920s; Morgan met him in 1930 at a boat-race party at Joe Ackerley's flat (see below), and formed an ardent friendship with him, which continued through Bob's marriage to May Hockey. Indeed he remained Forster's chief affection for the rest of his life. Bob became a probation officer, and in 1953 took up a post in Coventry. I knew him and May well.

5. Brian Remnant (1937–73); interviewed in 1956, came up to King's in 1958; read English, then Archaeology and Anthropology; became a teacher. Morgan had hopes of a close relationship with him.

6. The Unwritten Novel, ended as *The Other Boat*, a short story. It was finished in 1958 but remained unpublished. It was about a homosexual relationship across the colour bar, which would have been likely to offend conventional white people.

7. *Marianne Thornton*, the title of the biography of his aunt written by Forster and published in 1956. He was particularly proud of it.

8. Lionel and Cocoanut, the protagonists of *The Other Boat.*

9. The Cambridge Apostles are the secret intellectual discussion group founded in 1820. Its heyday was in the early twentieth century when Bertrand Russell, G.E. Moore, John Maynard Keynes and Morgan were all members. It still flourished in my day – in the next-door room.

10. Nadia Gray (1923–94), a Romanian film actress, best known for her role in

Federico Fellini's *La Dolce Vita*; Curzio Malaparte (1898–1957), Italian journalist, dramatist, short story writer and novelist, author of *La Pelle* (*The Skin*); Alberto Moravia (1907–90), Italian novelist, many of whose books were filmed. Best known in Britain for *The Woman of Rome* (*La Romana*).

11. Countess Elizabeth von Arnim (1866–1941), New Zealand-born novelist, famous for writing *Elizabeth and her German Garden*. Morgan was tutor to her five children in Nassenheide, Pomerania, in 1905.

12. I had to be taught to identify Italian obscenities by one of the servants.

13. Morgan was at Leiden University, in the Netherlands, to receive an honorary degree as a 'prominent man of letters'.

14. The Founder's Feast was in memory of Henry VI, who founded King's in 1441.

15. Noel Annan (1916–2000) became a fellow of King's in 1944 and a university lecturer in politics in 1947. In 1956 he was elected provost of King's at the age of thirty-nine. Later he became Lord Annan and the first full-time Chancellor of London University. He supervised me in Politics.

1957

16. Dorothy Parker (1893–1967), American poet and satirist, well-known for her sharp wit.

17. *The Paris Review*, a literary journal, was founded in Paris in 1953. It inaugurated a Writers at Work series of interviews with writers. Forster was the first writer to be interviewed, in the first issue, under the heading *The Art of Fiction*. As it happens, in 1954 I had tried to sell *The Paris Review* in the streets of Paris, for the editor, George Plimpton, an Old Kingsman and close friend of my brother. I also knew him well.

18. Garry Runciman, my oldest friend, with whom I attended Eton and Cambridge. An outstanding historical sociologist, who has been a Senior Research Fellow of Trinity College, Cambridge, since 1971. He succeeded his father as 3rd Viscount Runciman in 1989. He was president of the British Academy, 2001–4.

19. Schofield (sic) was A.F. Scholfield, who became Trinity librarian in 1919 and university librarian in 1923. He was elected a professorial fellow of King's. He had rooms in college immediately above Forster's. He died in 1970.

20. Arthur Cecil Pigou (1877–1957), fellow of King's from 1902, professor of Political Economy from 1908. A very distinguished economist. He had rooms beneath Forster's and was often to be seen on the lawn outside his staircase sitting in an old-fashioned seaside deckchair.

21. Norman Routledge (b.1928), mathematician and fellow of King's, 1951–60. Subsequently an assistant master at Eton.

22. Ian Stephens (1903–84), Indian civil servant and journalist, 1930–52, and a fellow of King's, 1952–8. He published a number of books.

23. The Elephanta caves were carved from rock in about the seventh century AD, on Elephanta Island in the harbour of Bombay (now Mumbai). They contain many beautiful sculptures, inspired by the worship of Shiva.

24. Mohammed el Adl was the Egyptian bus conductor with whom Forster had his first full sexual relationship in 1917. This was after he had written the unpublishable *Maurice* (1913–4). I assume 'The File of the Dead' to have been a cache of letters from friends who had died.

25. Rose Macaulay (1881–1958), novelist and essayist. She published the first critical book on Forster, *The Writings of E.M. Forster*, of which Forster did not have a high opinion, in 1938.

26. Stephen Spender (1909–95), poet, novelist and essayist.

27. The disagreeable landlady of our *pensione*.

28. Sir Nevile Bland was an Old Kingsman (1905–8), who was appointed Envoy Extraordinary and Minister Plenipotentiary to the Netherlands, 1938–48.

29. Stephen Spender.

30. E.K.Bennett, known as 'Francis' Bennett, was a student at the Working Men's College at which Forster taught. He later became a don at Gonville and Caius College and was one of Forster's closest friends in Cambridge after the Second World War.

31. J.R. (Joe) Ackerley (1896–1967); served on the Western Front in the First World War, and was interned in Switzerland; after the war went to Cambridge to work on becoming a writer; became a friend of Forster's when the latter wrote to him in April 1922 praising his poem *Ghosts* published in the *London Mercury*; Forster enabled him to become private secretary to the Maharajah of Chhatapur, which led to his memoir, *Hindoo Holiday*. 'Nick' I believe was Nick Furbank (b.1920), writer, scholar and critic, and Forster's chosen biographer.

32. G.M.Trevelyan; his wife, Janet, had died in 1956.

33. Ashok Desai (b.1936) was an Indian economist, whom I knew as a fellow undergraduate at King's. I believe that Morgan meant *veena*, one of several Indian plucked instruments.

34. 'I believe in aristocracy, though – if that is the right word, and if a democrat may use it. Not an aristocracy of power, based upon rank and influence, but an aristocracy of the sensitive, the considerate and the plucky. Its members are to be found in all nations and classes, and all through the ages, and there is a secret understanding between them when they meet. They represent the true human tradition, the one permanent victory of our queer race over cruelty and chaos. Thousands of them perish in obscurity, a few are great names. They are sensitive for others as well as for themselves, they are considerate without being fussy, their pluck is not swankiness but the power to endure, and they can take a joke.'

From 'What I Believe', published in *Two Cheers for Democracy*. I felt very much at home with this idea.

35. Benjamin Britten and Peter Pears.

1959

36. Jamini Roy (1887–1972), an extremely well-known Indian painter, who used traditional colours in his paintings of a rare simplicity. I was fortunate enough to be given by him three of his paintings.

37. George Savidis (1929–95) was a teacher, journalist, essayist, translator and critic; Charles Mauron (1899–1966) was a French translator and literary critic. He was Forster's translator and a good friend. His home at Saint-Rémy was a focal-point for many of the Bloomsbury group.

38. Billy Burrell, a fisherman friend of Britten's, in whose boat he and Forster used sometimes to go out.

39. The King's College Musical Society.

40. Vijay Lakhsmi Pandit (1900–90), known generally as Mrs Pandit, was the sister of India's first Prime Minister, Jawaharlal Nehru, and aunt of Indira Gandhi, Prime Minister for fifteen years. She was in effect head of India's most important political dynasty.

41. Professor Narayan Godbole is the Hindu at the centre of *Temple*, the final and most Indian part of *A Passage to India*.

42. Konarak is a small town in the Puri district of the state of Orissa, on the Bay of Bengal. It is the site of the thirteenth-century Sun Temple, which takes the form of the chariot of Surya the Sun God and is heavily decorated with stone carving.

43. Khajuraho, in Madhya Pradesh, has the largest group of Hindu and Jain temples, famous for their erotic sculptures.

44. A *puja* is a religious ritual performed as an offering by Hindus to various deities.

45. *Pather Panchali* was the film, the first of the Apur Trilogy, which launched the international career of Satyajit Ray.

46. Arthur Hibbert, University medieval historian

47. The third class carriages were absolutely packed, with people lying on the overhead luggage racks and very emaciated people lying under the seats.

48. The Ajanta caves in Maharashtra are twenty-nine rock-cut cave monuments, which contain paintings and sculptures which are masterpieces of Buddhist religious art. At the archaeological site at Ellora, also in Maharashtra, the finest site for Indian rock-cut architecture, are twelve Buddhist, seventeen Hindu and five Jain 'caves' – in fact structures excavated out of the vertical face of the Charanandri hills. Morgan, on visiting Ellora in 1913, told Masood 'the caves are cruel, obscene things, the work of

146

devils, but very wonderful' (also quoted in Beauman, op.cit.) In 1945 Morgan finally visited the Ajanta caves, which he had missed in 1913 and 1922.

49. Francis Haskell (1928–2000), art historian and fellow of King's from 1954.

50. Michael Jaffe (1923–97), art historian, became a fellow of King's in 1952 and held his first appointment in the History of Art Department in 1956.

51. Rob and Silvia had two sons, Clive and Paul.

52. Carlos van Hasselt, born in Holland in 1929, was a senior member of King's and Assistant Keeper of Prints and Drawings at the Fitzwilliam Museum, 1956–62.

53. Characters in *The Longest Journey*.

54. Lindsay Heather (b.1937); choral scholar at King's, 1957–60, later a freelance singer and choral conductor. Morgan had hopes of a close relationship with him.

55. Mary Eleanor Mayle, Forster's mother's sister.

1961

56. Forster's host and hostess were Commander Sir Michael Culme-Seymour, RN, fifth baronet (1909–99) and Lady Faith Culme-Seymour (1911–83), daughter of the ninth Earl of Sandwich. I cannot trace how Forster came to know them, although I believe it was through Lord Sandwich.

57.. *A Passage to India*, dramatised by Santha Rama Rau (1923-2009), with Forster's approval.

58. Now hangs in the Britten-Pears Library at Aldeburgh.

59. 'Nor Land that Liris, silent river / Nibbles away with its sleepy water'. Horace, *Odes* Book 1.31.7

60. The Evelyn Hospital, a Cambridge Nursing Home.

61. An Old Kingsman and a doctor, living in Cambridge, who was often consulted by fellows of King's on medical matters.

62. Paul Anthony Tanner (1935–98) was one of the foremost critics of American literature in the period from Henry James to modern times.

63. My older brother (later Sir) Andrew Leggatt, a distinguished lawyer.

64. Donald Beves (1896–1961), fellow of King's from 1924, University Lecturer in French, 1930–46.

65. Alex Kwapong (b.1927) a Ghanaian classics student at King's, 1948–51. Later professor of Classics 1962–6, vice-chancellor of the University of Ghana 1966–76, and vice-rector, United Nations University. I got to know him in Ghana.

66. Frank Adcock (1886–1968) became a Fellow of King's in 1912. He was Cambridge Professor of Ancient History, 1925–51.

67. Rob Buckingham's wife.

68. My family home in Long Sutton, Hampshire.

69. Nicholas Kaldor (1908–86) was one of the foremost Cambridge economists of the

post-war period. He advised several governments, including the Ghana government in 1961–2, during which time I got to know him.

70. Peter Paul Rubens' 1634 painting, *The Adoration of the Magi*, was presented to the college by Major Alfred Allnatt (1889–1969) in 1961. It is placed in the east end of the Chapel as the altarpiece.

71. Angus McPherson (1916–2000) became a fellow of King's in 1942 and first bursar 1951–62, when he became treasurer of Cambridge University and later registrary (chief officer of the council of the senate).

72. David Holbrook, poet, novelist and literary critic, was a fellow of King's, 1961–5.

73. Eric Fletcher, a graduate of King's in 1948, who had taught in the Cambridge area for the previous four years and was about to leave the area to take up a post at Keighley Technical College, in 1959.

74. Philip Noel-Baker (1889–1982) was an Old Kingsman, who was much involved in the formation of the League of Nations. He was a Labour MP, 1936–70, and an Olympic runner for Britain in the games of 1912, 1920 and 1924. He was a famous campaigner for disarmament who won the Nobel Prize for Peace in 1959.

75. Zia Mohyeddin (b.1933), a Pakistani actor.

76. Eric Portman (1901–68), a distinguished stage and film actor.

77. Dame Gladys Cooper (1888–1971), an actress whose career spanned seven decades on stage, television and film. The exclamation mark may have been because of her age, seventy-three. However, she continued to work until she was 82.

78. Giuseppe Tomasi di Lampedusa (1896–1957) wrote just one novel, *Il Gattopardo*, published posthumously in 1958. He was a favourite of Forster's.

79. Abinger in Surrey, where Edward (Eddie), Forster's father, had built a house for his wife, Lily, in due course to be called West Hackhurst.

1962

80. Hugh Meredith, mostly referred to as H.O.M., whom Forster in his early Cambridge period thought was the cleverest by far of all his contemporaries. He influenced Forster as he loved to *épater* the narrow-minded, but he was also a cynic, whom Forster later blamed for infecting all his friends with his pessimism. He was Professor of Economics at Queen's University, Belfast, 1911–45.

81. I went to Sierra Leone on Longmans' business, to the university and secondary schools. I even flew to Bo in the smallest plane I have ever known.

82. Robert Thornton, Marianne Thornton's uncle.

83. Jonathan Miller, trained as a doctor, is one of the world's leading theatre and opera directors, author, sculptor, photographer, television presenter and humorist. He came to prominence in 1960 and onwards in the comedy review *Beyond the Fringe,* with Peter Cook, Alan Bennett and Dudley Moore. A close friend.

84. Political and Economic Planning, formed in 1931, was a non-governmental policy think tank and planning organisation, financed by corporations. In 1978 it was absorbed into the Policy Studies Institute (PSI).

85. The ninth earl of Sandwich had died on 15 June 1962. He was the father of Faith, who married Commander Sir Michael Culme-Seymour. See n. 56.

86. The first part of a history of Forster's involvement with West Hackhurst and the surrounding area, from his aunt Laura's time onwards.

87. *The Torque* was a short story, a fantasy, set in pre-historical time, which was anti-religious, with an element of homosexuality. Unpublished in Forster's lifetime.

88. Alison Leggatt (1904–90), my aunt, a fine character actress.

89. Arthur Cole (1883–1968), educated at King's, a noted bibliophile, who gave the Rowe Music Library to the College.

90. Mattei Radev (1927–2009), a Bulgarian, who arrived in London as a stowaway in 1950 and became a very talented picture-framer. He was an attractive young man, who had many homosexual relationships, including one with Forster that lasted many years. He inherited a noteworthy art collection of 800 works from Eardley Knollys (1902–91), artist, art critic and collector, who was bequeathed it by Eddy Sackville-West (1901–65), music critic and novelist.

1963

91. Robert Birley (1903-82), Headmaster of Eton 1949-63, strongly opposed to apartheid, was taking up a visiting professorship at the University of Witwatersrand in Johannesburg, 1964–7. He was my Headmaster and history teacher.

92. Maimie was Forster's father Edward's cousin. T.E. Lawrence (1888–1935), archaeologist and author, was best known for his liaison role during the Arab revolt against Ottoman Turkish rule, 1916–8, as 'Lawrence of Arabia'. Bapu Sahib refers to the Maharajah of Dewas. Bone is Henry Bone, the gardener whom the Forsters inherited when they lived at West Hackhurst. Syed Ross Masood, a great Muslim patriot, was tutored in Latin by Forster before going up to Oxford. He became a close and influential friend, one of 'masterful personality and charm'. It was a true affair of the heart. Frank Vicary was a young naval rating whom Forster met in Alexandria in 1916; they remained friends after the war. He died in 1956.

93. 'In the name of God', a simplified version of the normal 'in the name of the Father, the Son and the Holy Ghost'.

94. He refers to his maternal grandmother, Louisa Graham Whichelo.

95. I think this means something like 'breathed over'.

96. An Australian who was a very well-known sexologist.

97. Hugh Walpole (1884–1941), a New Zealander, was educated in England and lived in Cumbria. He was a very successful author, publishing his first novel in 1909.

98. Marcel Proust (1871–1922). The reference is of course to *A la recherche du temps perdu*. I have never understood Forster's point, since I don't know that this practice was seen as derogatory of Proust.

99. My family home, Parsonage Farm (see n. 68).

100. Ed Shils (1910–95), an outstanding American sociologist, from the University of Chicago, who advised and supported me to undertake graduate study for a Ph.D. in sociology at Chicago.

101. William Plomer (1903–73) was a South African novelist, poet and literary editor. He was Benjamin Britten's librettist for *Gloriana*.

102. A reference to my fiancée, never said to me.

103. Desmond Shawe-Taylor (1907–95), music critic.

104. Mrs Failing in *The Longest Journey*.

105. The Provost's Lodge at King's.

106. Angus Wilson (1913–91), novelist and short story writer.

107. The British Museum.

108. I think this is the point, after noting Morgan's poor opinion of Noel, to state clearly that Noel was always extremely friendly and helpful to me whenever I sought his advice, right up to the years when I was senior tutor of King's, 1973–81.

109. I.A. Richards (1893–1979), celebrated as the author of *Principles of Literary Criticism* and *Practical Criticism*. He came with his wife, Dorothy Pilley.

110. Mstislav Rostropovitch (1927–2007), the famous Russian cellist and conductor.

111. Eric Crozier (1914–94), co-founder with Britten of the Aldeburgh Festival (1948), was an experienced librettist who collaborated on Britten's *Albert Herring* and helped Forster with the libretto of *Billy Budd*.

112. Reg Palmer seems to have been the name by which Arthur Barnet, a Weybridge bus driver, with whom he had a brief relationship, was known to Forster.

113. Britten's three-act opera with a libretto by William Plomer, based on Lytton Strachey's *Elizabeth and Essex*.

114. The Earl of Harewood (1923–2011) was Managing Director and later Chairman of the English National Opera. He co-authored for more than thirty years *Kobbe's Complete Opera Book*.

115. Paul Cadmus (1904–99), an American artist, best known for his paintings and drawings of nude male figures. He did an excellent drawing of Morgan.

116. Citizens, friends of the Buckinghams.

1964

117. Frank Iredale, ex-Metropolitan Police, became head porter in my first year at King's in 1954.

118. Eric Fletcher, married in 1955, was in process of divorce. He remarried in 1966.

119. I left the marriage in 1986 and was divorced in 1991.

120. Tolstoy's novella *The Death of Ivan Ilyich* is a devastating story in which Ilyich, who has lived his life according to the 'perfect propriety in external observances required by public opinion', as a result, suffers a lingering illness in severe physical and mental pain and in dread fear of death, because he has lived his life wrongly.

121. Jayant Narliker (b.1938) graduated from Cambridge and studied for his Ph.D. in astrophysics under Fred Hoyle. He was a Fellow of King's, 1964–72, and a founder member of the Institute of Theoretical Astronomy in Cambridge, 1966–72.

122. Kenneth Harrison left his King's fellowship in 1960, to become Professor of Biochemistry at the University of Tehran. He returned to England in 1963 and thereafter lived in London and then in Cumbria.

123. Forster inherited the lease of West Hackhurst from Laura Forster (1839–1924) in 1924.

124. Cyril Fielding in *A Passage to India*.

125. Figsbury Rings, an ancient monument five miles north-east of Salisbury, which partly inspired *The Longest Journey*.

126. Mattei Radev had been arrested 'without cause', beaten up by policemen in a police car, and denied access to a doctor. He subsequently sent Forster a postcard from Luxor in September.

127. Jack is W.J.H. Sprott (1897–1971), nicknamed 'Sebastian' and 'Jack', a friend of Morgan from the 1920s onwards, who taught at University College, Nottingham, eventually becoming professor of Philosophy. He was Morgan's executor briefly, between Morgan's death and his own. He and Joe took a holiday in Italy in September 1964.

128. The rebuilding in King's, to begin in 1965, was quite massive and would be going on in and near Forster's part of the college. The King's Annual Report of 1964 warned that there would be 'a period of some noise and discomfort'.

129. Hugh Meredith died on 31 July 1964 in Oxford, where he had lived since 1957, when he married his third wife, presumably the 'Peggy' mentioned on 4 August.

130. Norman Scarfe (b.1923) was the editor/author of a number of Shell Guides to various regions of Britain. He lived at Shingle Street, near Aldeburgh in Suffolk.

131. Heather had a three year award 'for operatic study'.

132. We amused ourselves to think that our waiter in Vicenza looked exactly like Sir Adrian Boult, who famously conducted the BBC Symphony Orchestra and the London Philharmonic Orchestra.

133. Chetwynd Court was just off our staircase, leading to the College kitchens.

134. Professor Morris Janowitz (1919–88), a distinguished American sociologist, especially for his work on the sociology of the military and on sociological theory, was my hard-driving mentor at the University of Chicago.

135. The *Missa Solemnis* in D major was composed 1819–23. It ends with the *Gloria*.

136. Kenneth (later Lord) Clark, always known as K. He was Director of the National

Gallery, 1934–45, Slade Professor of Fine Art at Oxford, 1946–50 and 1961–2, and Chairman of the Arts Council, 1953–60. He and his wife Jane lived at Saltwood Castle in Kent.

137. This well-known remark is taken by many to refer to Forster not writing any novels after *A Passage to India*. It does not in my view. See Afterword.

1965

138. David Willcocks (b.1919), university lecturer in music; organist, master of the choristers and fellow of King's 1957–74. Later director of the Royal College of Music.
139. Webbs Court, in King's.
140. *Howard's End*.

1966

141. Edmund Leach (1910–89), one of the leading social anthropologists of the English-speaking world. Joined the Cambridge Department of Anthropology in 1953, became a reader in 1957 and a fellow of King's in 1960. He was professor in 1972 and provost of King's, 1966–79. In 1973 I became his senior tutor.
142. Papworth Hospital, specialising in cardiac surgery, ten miles west of Cambridge.
143. I do not know what lies behind this attitude.
144. Mrs Richardson, who started as a bedmaker in 1960.
145. I suddenly had some problems with my hands – i.e. I couldn't write. This was said to be due to overwork. It did not last long.

1967

146. Quentin Bell (1910–96), the son of Clive and Vanessa Bell, was professor of art history or fine art at various universities and finally at Sussex University (1967–76), where I knew him during my tenure there (1966–73). He wrote an outstanding biography of his famous aunt, Virginia Woolf.
147. Ackerley was found dead in his bed on the morning of 4 June 1967. He was seventy.

1968

148. I believe it was the vice-provost, Edward Shire.
149. P.N. Furbank, *E.M.Forster: A Life,* Volume Two (Secker & Warburg, 1978).

150. Furbank quotes Morgan's letter to T. E. Lawrence of 18 March 1927. The tale is from Herodotus' *History*, Book 3, Chapter 40.

151. See Furbank, p. 132.

152. Wendy Moffat, *A Great Unrecorded History: A New Life of E.M. Forster* (Farrar, Straus and Giroux, 2010) p. 75

153. Frank Kermode, *Concerning E.M. Forster*. His long essay in this, 'E.M. Forster: A Causerie' is more subtle and intelligent than anything else written about Forster.

154. He wrote over 400 pieces – short stories, essays, articles, reviews and broadcasts.

155. Stuart Hampshire writes that Forster sees individuals and personal relations against 'the surrounding natural order sublime, unknown, unlimited, not understood'. In *The New York Review of Books*, Volume 6, Number 8, 12 May 1966.

156. Quoted by Kermode, p. 82

157. *A Passage to India* (Edward Arnold, 1957), p. 323

158. I refer to this on p. 27, and it is why I included my experience of the worship of the goddess Kali (see pp. 29–31) to show something of an alternative acquaintanceship with Hinduism.

159. David Lean directed the film *A Passage to India* in 1984.

160. Kermode (p. 129) quotes Forster as believing that 'art was "the one orderly product" to set against muddle'.

161. Both quotations are from 'Art for Art's Sake' in *Two Cheers for Democracy* (Edward Arnold, 1951), pp. 102, 104.

162. 'What I Believe' in *Two Cheers for Democracy*, p. 79.

163. *A Passage to India*, p.336.

HESPERUS PRESS

Hesperus Press is committed to bringing near what is far – far both in space and time. Works written by the greatest authors, and unjustly neglected or simply little known in the English-speaking world, are made accessible through new translations and a completely fresh editorial approach. Through these classic works, the reader is introduced to the greatest writers from all times and all cultures.

For more information on Hesperus Press, please visit our website: **www.hesperuspress.com**